PSYCHOLOGY OF ATTRACTION

How to Become More Attractive to Others Via the Power of Positive Thinking and Developing a Clearly Defined Life Mission (2022 Guide for Beginners)

Moira Davidson

Table of Contents

Understanding Oneself

Most people, regrettably, do not utilize their full potential or ability. Ask any self-development guru or look at any research on human potential. There is a lot more of what you have than what you are currently utilizing. You must develop a deeper relationship with yourself to realize your full potential and draw in your true calling.

Do the majority of us even understand what our true potential is? Many people don't! Have you come close to realizing your full potential?

Sadly, the majority of people are unaware of their potential. They become comfortable in their daily routine cycle and fall into it over time without ever realizing that they are capable of much more than what they are doing at the time. We fail to reach our full potential because of time and other limitations. Unlocking your real potential is fundamental to your living. If you are going about your life in a mechanical way, you simply exist, you do not live.

To truly live, you have to explore deeper into yourself and discover your true potential. One of the biggest regrets a person can have in his or her life is never to have discovered their real calling or unlocked their fullest potential. The most painful words at the far end of your life are probably, "could have." Eliminate the "could have" from your life by taking control of your life right now.

Here are some tips to help you unlock your true potential.

Explore possibilities and your full potential.

Irrespective of your inborn talents, family background, or wealth, as well as breaks and opportunities, realize your full potential. This is most likely the decisive factor in every success story. It often happens that the underdog who became one of the most popular and looked up inspirational figures will be the one who discovered his or her potential and believed in it even when others refused to.

Successful people have learned the fine art of tapping into their fullest potential to live the life of their dreams. We have always wondered why despite being equally talented, skilled, educated, and experienced as other persons, we have not been able to accomplish the level of success this person has witnessed. Ever wondered why?

Those persons have successfully discovered or tapped into their potential to create the life of their dreams.

Take for instance that you had the best car with the slickest gear to take you anywhere you want to go. You always have a map to guide you toward your destination. However, in this case, you don't know where you want to go. You don't know what you want to achieve or accomplish in life. If you don't know where you want to go in life or what you want to accomplish, how will you get there? And how will you know what you want to accomplish until you realize your fullest potential?

Only when you realize your fullest potential can you set high goals for yourself, and actively work toward fulfilling those goals. Right now, you have a map and a car but no destination in sight. This makes the process of goal fulfillment almost impossible. You can start driving, but it will be driving aimlessly.

How does a person discover their fullest potential? It can be a long and frustrating process, but it's worth pursuing. Begin by avoiding negative individuals and focusing on what you enjoy doing or are good at. Explore ideas and options until you discover something you truly enjoy doing and which doesn't seem like work.

For some people finding their calling is instinctive. It will happen when they are clicking a picture. They will suddenly realize that taking images makes them happy, which suggests that becoming a skilled photographer is their genuine calling or potential. Others will have the good fortune to have their skill discovered by a diligent parent or instructor at a young age (we have all seen these young protégés, haven't we?).

These kids can become success stories if they are fortunate enough to have their genuine skills identified and developed at a young age. One of the most regrettable aspects of negativity is that it enters our unconscious thinking without our awareness.

Then, without our knowledge, it spreads like poison into our subconscious.

Get Rid of the Negative

Avoid letting your or other people's negativity get the better of you. Your prospects of achieving your full potential may be hampered. If you want to be in charge of your destiny, learn how to control both your own and other people's energy. Due to the negativity in their environment, some people may struggle for a long time to recognize their calling or genuine potential. Stop around yourself with people who kill your dreams and drain your energy as the first step toward realizing your full potential.

The Effect on the Environment

Think for a moment about the following inquiries.

- What natural talents, abilities, and skills do I possess?

- What am I truly good at or excel at? • In what areas can I use my strengths most effectively?

- Where can I apply my values?

- Where might my abilities be useful?

- What gives me genuine comfort?

- What causes me to feel genuine happiness?

- What do I enjoy doing even if I'm not getting compensated for it?

Pay attention to your passions and the things that make you feel fulfilled on the inside.

Determine Your Areas of Strength, Values, and Passion

It is simpler to understand your actual calling and fulfill your potential if you have identified your values, strengths, personality, and passions. Understanding your passion and realizing your highest potential are inextricably linked.

On the other hand, our passion frequently results from our innate qualities, talents, and characteristics. Finding your strengths, values, personality, and other traits is crucial to realizing your greatest potential.

Say you have the good fortune to identify your passions. When you discover something you enjoy doing, you will work on it with heart and intention. This provides you the drive to pursue your ideal life or your goals and the spirit to overcome any barriers in your way.

Open Your Mind's Power

The most powerful tool in the cosmos is our intellect. The world can be won or conquered by those who can win the mental battle. It has limitless possibilities. Your ideas can be reprogrammed for success if you begin to comprehend the power of your mind and become a master of the universe's laws.

What, in your opinion, do the majority of transformational and personal development coaches do to inspire their clients to succeed? They don't possess a success-guaranteed magic wand. They merely make an effort to rewire their thinking to adopt a success mindset.

Each of us has an infinitely flexible brain, but not everyone makes the most of it. Imagine your mind as a supercomputer or more like a thumb drive. It contains all the information you gather from your senses. The subconscious mind absorbs whatever you put into it, good or bad, and, like the genie in the famous story, grants every request that comes into its domain.

See how effective our subconscious mind is at helping us achieve our objectives. It must be fed repeatedly into the subconscious mind until it solidifies into an image that can be translated into reality. Whether or whether something is genuine, your subconscious mind will accept it as real if you think about it frequently. To assist you in achieving the goal, it will then work with you and for you.

Change your negative self-talk to optimistic thoughts. Keep a careful and mindful eye on your self-talk. If you notice that your inner critic is taking control, gradually replace it with an optimistic and helpful one.

For instance, "I may not be perfect at this, but I am eager to work toward mastering it, and very soon I will" can be used instead of "I am terrible at this" or "I can never do this properly."

By enhancing your current abilities or learning new ones, you can learn to get over your anxieties of never being good enough. To increase your confidence, let go of social phobias or nervousness and engage more in social situations. Get rid of self-limiting and negative beliefs since they will nastily infiltrate your mind and shape your reality.

Embrace Chances for Growth

Seize chances for personal development. Even if they are not immediately apparent, possibilities for personal improvement are constantly present. If your manager asks you to take on more responsibility or move to a different area, don't think of it as more work. Consider it a chance to learn new talents.

We can often prevent ourselves from pursuing fresh chances that promote personal growth because we are afraid of change.

Outside of your comfort zone, success awaits. If you want to achieve the extraordinary, learn to push the boundaries and go the additional mile. Ordinary actions will not produce amazing results! Learn to recognize new chances and have the insight to understand how they might advance your personal development.

Develop a Clear Sense of Purpose

To activate the law of attraction, you must deliberately and intently focus on the outcome you want in your life. You need to have a distinct sense of purpose and direction if you want to achieve success in life and reach your goals. You need to be aware of your goals and where you are going in life. Every creative deed or accomplishment starts with a dream or vision held by someone. The path becomes simple if you are clear on what you want to accomplish in life or where you want to go. You can find the direction by setting your compass.

Set goals that appear unattainable or that you never thought you could achieve and work diligently, purposefully, and mindfully to achieve these 'impossible' goals. Never undervalue your ability to influence this world.

The key to starting to activate the law of attraction is to value yourself and your ability. Remember that to attract something into your life, you must first think that it already exists. Before you can materialize something, you must first think that you are deserving of getting it.

Be ready for difficulties. Be the person who welcomes challenges and sees them as stepping stones that get you closer to your objective rather than as obstacles to overcome. Don't follow conventional wisdom. Do not take someone else's assertion that something cannot be done as fact. You should always keep in mind that when someone claims something cannot be done, they are referring to their world, not yours. Don't let anyone dictate to you what is possible. Aim for the unattainable, and you will succeed.

Goal: Live a Balanced Life

Aim to live a balanced life where all aspects of your health—mental, emotional, spiritual, physical, financial, personal, and professional—are in perfect harmony. This will enable you to lead a life that is more rewarding, satisfying, and full. Avoid concentrating too much on one aspect of your life. Wealth accumulation is as crucial as spiritual growth. Living a balanced and fulfilling life puts you in a better state of mind, which makes it easier for you to attract more of what you want.

Don't fall head over heels for the notion of ease. Be audacious, accomplished, and fulfilled instead.

Identify Your Passion

There is a proverb that states, "If you enjoy what you do for a living, you will never work a day in your life." It couldn't have been explained any better. Possessing a single-minded love for your work is the key to achieving tremendous success in it. It can help to be intelligent, have the proper connections, be persistent, lucky, and brave. But nothing compares to passion.

Any successful individual may be recognized by one thing in particular: their love for what they do. It is rare to achieve greatness in any undertaking without a substantial amount of passion for it. Investigate your passion before establishing goals. What intrinsic passion do you have? What occupation brings you joy? When you do something, what doesn't feel like work? What activities bring you inner serenity and happiness? What activities involve work yet help you unwind and decompress?

If you want to achieve great things in your life, find your passion. Make the most of this desire. Use it to focus on your vision, objectives, and dreams. Your odds of manifesting success or achieving your goals increase the more you follow your passions.

Once more, doing what you love every day sends extremely potent good frequencies into the cosmos. Your good ideas, deeds, words, and intentions, which naturally arise when you are passionate about what you do, influence these positive energies. The cosmos responds to this optimism by sending back a frequency that matches it, which increases the amount of positivity in your life.

The contagious joyful energy that results from living the life of your desires spreads like wildfire. People want to be around positive thought leaders who inspire them and give them a feeling of direction. It's a great circle of optimism. You discover your passion or purpose by accident and take pleasure in your work. Then it spreads to others who feel your strong sense of positivity, purpose, and intention, which in turn causes them to draw in more positivity. Therefore, even if you are unaware of it, your passion affects not just you but also people who are close to you.

Imagine you work as an interior decorator and designer. If you are truly excited about your profession, your ideas, opinions, and creativity will come through when you chat with people about decorating their homes! People will be drawn to you based on how you present your views and recommendations. People either possess passion or do not; it is difficult to fake. People are more complimentary about your work when they can see your passion. This optimism shows itself as more work and greater achievement coming your way. This passion is crucial to your success and achieving your objectives.

What inspires you? Where do you get your motivation? Consider the top five individuals you spend the most time with. What do these people do exactly? What do they love to do? What goes through their minds? Do they inspire and motivate you to pursue your goals? Do these people motivate you to try your hardest? You can discover your life's purpose by identifying what motivates you the most. For instance, you might need a lot of cash. But that's not the main reason you're here. You can desire a large sum of money to travel around and experience many cultures. You might need more money if you want to follow your calling and satisfy your desire to explore the world.

Some people's true calling in life is to provide for their families. The desire to give their family a happy life drives all of their decisions. Others define true financial freedom as having the time and resources to spend with their loved ones. It might help further a cause you care deeply about. The "how" won't ever be a problem if your "why" is obvious. The show will become clear if you are clear on why you want to do something. You'll get closer to your goal if your "why" is compelling. Permit yourself to set seemingly impossible goals and to savor the satisfaction of seeing those goals come true.

Every one of us has unique aspirations, aspirations, visions, purposes, and objectives in life. Never contrast your goals with those of others.

Our life's journey is directed by the purpose we each carry inside of us. Just picture what a great place the world would be if everyone lived according to their genuine purpose.

Faith System

According to Abraham Hicks, a belief is a notion that you tend to think over and over again. Multiple beliefs lead to a multiplicity of ingrained beliefs. That is the way you think. Your daily general thoughts—sort of like a routine—make up your thinking. The majority of your beliefs are simply replayed thoughts that have been lodged in your mind since you were a little child.

When we are young, we are like sponges. We observe and imitate the people who raise us, and because of the things they say and do, we naturally adopt their beliefs. What kids, we don't know any different, so we do as others do. We come to perceive life through their eyes and anticipate that it will play out in the same way, whether they are wealthy or not.

Consider racism as an example. Racism is something that develops in youngsters as a result of their surroundings. On the other hand, certain beliefs develop over time as a result of life experiences, particularly traumatic events since they have a stronger emotional component. As a type of survival mechanism, traumatic experiences linger with us more than positive ones do, allowing us to learn what triggers them and what can prevent them from happening again.

Our viewpoint, how we perceive people, how we speak and think, as well as how we construct our sense of self-worth, are all shaped by our beliefs or habitual ideas. As a result, some people consistently experience good fortune because they act, think, and speak positively about their lives. Some people experience extended periods of bad luck because they believe they are unworthy of good things, complain a lot, and are likely grumpy most of the time. Wealthy people may be wealthy because that is all they think about and care about; they do not need to be joyful or optimistic to be wealthy.

Our subconscious, and consequently our future and expectations of life, are shaped by the mindset we adopt from life. Throughout a person's life, their beliefs will be frequently demonstrated to them. For instance, if a person grew up in a very impoverished family and their parents taught them that wealth was terrible and only obtained by bad people. Due to being taught that this is how life is, the child will grow up in poverty and hate those who have wealth. Even if a family is poor, if the parents teach their kids to believe in themselves and aim high, they will probably grow up to be prosperous.

Ideas are seeds, and while we are young, our subconscious mind is a fertile field where ideas are just ready to sprout.

You must learn to comprehend how you think and see yourself if you want to start altering your life's course and using the LOA to your advantage. Your self-image, which in turn shapes your outlook on life, is a reflection of your mindset or subconscious. Your self-concept influences how you view the world. You view the world through lenses that are tinted, which do not accurately reflect reality but rather your views that you hold to be true.

Do you believe you deserve wonderful goods, good relationships, and a well-paying job? Simply observing your surroundings, the people in your life, your bank account, your car, your clothes, and the conversations you have will reveal your mindset or image. You must realize that the vibrations you give off through your everyday thoughts, feelings, visualizations, actions, and speech represent who you are, what you usually think about, how you feel about yourself, and how your life reflects those vibrations.

It's crucial to take a step back and consider your life objectively. Avoid judging yourself; it only prevents change. By taking the time to make the connections, you will begin the transformation toward a more rewarding life. Additionally, it takes care of something crucial for you that you might not be aware of right away. A more objective view of your existence increases self-awareness. Change requires awareness since ignorance is blinding. You can see more clearly when you're aware.

Understanding how you draw experiences and things into your life will help you make the connection between yourself and the world around you. Knowledge is power. Many people are incredibly oblivious to who they are and how the mirror of life reflects their actions. They are cut off from themselves and can only perceive the world as completely apart from them. This may lead to intense rage and depression. Being shut off from oneself is the same as being cut off from reality, which can be quite upsetting and depressing.

The best place to start connecting how you think, speak, and behave to the outside world is by realizing how your reality reflects you. A great place to start is by trying to recognize when you are speaking negatively to yourself. The first step in reducing negative self-talk and changing it to something more positive is to recognize it. especially when you're debating with imaginary friends. If you argue with someone in your head, the next time you see them, that negativity will inevitably come out of you. Making up arguments in your head will increase the likelihood of them happening.

It is up to us to recognize how we view life and to stop arguing with other people in our minds. Do you have a negative outlook on things in your life, such as money, love, health, or work? Do you anticipate bad things happening? Are you anticipating the arrival of the other shoe? Do you worry all the time? Do you frequently express dissatisfaction with your life? How do you feel after overspending your budget? Do you feel bad about going above and above for yourself? You need to ask yourself whether your beliefs about life are actually facts or merely acquired opinions.

Understanding your perspective and recognizing the unpleasant moments is a crucial first step. That makes it possible to adapt. Try to examine your mental image of others. Are you only kind to some people when you meet them face-to-face but have negative thoughts about them otherwise? This self-defeating internal dialogue only serves to hinder you; it emits unfavorable vibrations that prevent you from obtaining what you desire.

You're thinking about it. Consequently, producing a negative feeling produces negative energy that may have negative repercussions. Including the body's release of stress hormones, which can make you feel sicker and angrier. Take a deep breath, learn to let go of the throttle, dial back the negativity, and practice shifting your focus to good thoughts.

to self-esteem-boosting ideas. You must develop a more self-centered attitude toward the way your thoughts affect how you feel.

Try to feel thankful for the people you love more often rather than dwelling on the people who irritate you.

The LOA seems absurd to most people when they first learn about it, but what is absurd is that unhappy people spend the majority of their days stressing and worrying about unfavorable outcomes. many of which never materialize. I mean, isn't that just plain absurd? Little do they realize the harm they are causing themselves. If thoughts can become reality, why wouldn't negative things also? you could ask. Thoughts that are consistently practiced usually come true.

Most people worry about various issues left and right and don't give most of their thoughts adequate time to develop. Since they rarely appear, most fresh notions.

Instinctual World

All of your beliefs, all of your memories, and possibly even all of the world's and all prior lives are stored in your subconscious. Your mentality is rooted in it.

You have less conscious power over your life than your subconscious does.

The software that runs your brain and life is called the subconscious, and it is where the programs that control your life are kept. You run your subconscious programs every day; these are your habits. The conscious mind is where software programs are executed.

You must be adamant about it if you want to change your subconscious using your consciousness. To improve or expand the programs, you'll need time, perseverance, patience, and a burning ambition for innovation. An entirely new program can only enter your waking experience once it has developed in your subconscious. Your mind's interior obscurity is a creative haven. For them to develop into beliefs, they need to be nurtured and loved on frequently.

developing new beliefs

Everything we think, believe, and perceive about the world is within our skulls.

by keeping an eye on your surroundings, your thoughts, and the things you say out loud. You can see the energy you're expending. Most people alive today—98% of the population—are unwittingly exploiting their God-given powers of attraction to lead unhappy, sick lifestyles.

Most individuals simply respond when something bad happens to them or when they see something on the news. Most people simply compare themselves to others and long for a different life.

Additionally, the majority of people that gather with others gossip, whine and restate the negative things that are happening in their lives to one another. Depending on how badly your day is going, all these behaviors either cause your vibration frequency to remain the same or cause it to decrease.

For the most part, this behavior appears to be normal, but it is precisely this behavior that represents a misuse of the authority that has been granted to us. Thought becomes tangible through speech. The charge you make grows stronger when you complain to another person because someone else, another awareness, now accepts what you're saying. As a result, in their reality, they will likewise associate you with that complaint, which further cements the negativity in your reality.

Stopping your whining is extremely important since the less you can talk about the bad things, the less you're thinking about them. Therefore, less of it will manifest in your reality. To some extent, it's beneficial to let things out, but only if they are seriously upsetting you.

It's a good idea to express such feelings once or twice just to get them out when you can't stop thinking about them. like a balloon about to pop releasing its air pressure. However, if you keep saying that, you'll only keep drawing bad things into your life.

You must acquire new ways to communicate, think, feel, and see. You must start here to develop your ideas and to be original for your own sake. It is your life's purpose to be the one who creates it. Affirmations are useful in this situation. Affirmations are tools that can be used to guide the mind in a positive direction, which is the starting point for the remainder of our life. Because our ideas come before every decision we make, they reflect the caliber of our lives.

Every thought you have has an impact on your reality; it is a statement you make about yourself that raises your vibration or degree of attraction.

Even if you're thinking about someone else, it's still all about you. Whatever is going on in your head, whether it's positive or negative and aimed at someone else, only you and the energy you emit as a result of the emotions connected to those thoughts are affected. The biggest toll on the person with a negative attitude is themselves.

Have you ever taken a step back and considered your audience? You are. The brain in you! One way to view your ideas is as instructions from your brain to your body. Your body will begin to feel tense and your heart will begin to pound if you are upset with your boss. Your brain receives furious thoughts, which causes you to feel tense and uneasy. To make the rage feel more physical, your brain will release the necessary hormones.

Do you not start to think about autoimmune disorders as a result?

"Holding on to anger is like grabbing a hot coal and tossing it at someone else; you get burned."

Buddha

Because of this, just you and not anyone else will suffer from the effects of any negative ideas. The emotions that result from bad thoughts will also come from you, which will make those close to you feel the same way about you. If you consistently have a bad attitude, it will also show up in your vibration, attracting more bad people, situations, and experiences.

Even those who are normally upbeat can become hostile to you if you manage to evoke their negative emotions. After that, they will leave you and wonder what the heck just occurred.

Similar results apply to positive emotions; you will draw out the best qualities in those with whom you contact. People you love won't ever hurt you, but because of how much you care for them, you can't recognize their bad qualities. Think about giving yourself some time to reflect.

How often do you complain or become irate in your head before taking into account how your day has gone? Do you observe a connection between the outside world and the thoughts you have?

Pay close attention to the differences in the way those you like treat you and the way those you don't like treat you.

Consider how far into the remainder of your week that terrible day trickles if you are having a bad day.

We were endowed with the capacity for desire and the capability of imagination because we are creators. It is up to us to define who we are and how we want to conduct our lives, letting go of outdated notions that were imposed on us by the outside world. Every person has a dream that was given to them for them to fully embody and express their true selves. The joy we continually aspire to infuse our lives with is what we receive when we realize our dreams; it naturally occurs when we follow our passion. Nothing is too big to dream.

It all begins with choosing to think thoughts that are more beneficial to you and dedicating time each day to doing so. Eventually, this choice will become ingrained in your mind, and you will have a new mindset. To think fresh thoughts is to live new lives. To start, you must choose what you eventually want to be, have, and do. to approach it from several angles and to add details as if you were writing a tale about your life. This brings us to the process of thinking, which is how your world is first created.

The effects of thought on overall wellbeing

The human body is a fragile instrument. As a mind-follower, it acts by mental commands. The command must follow the instructions, whether it is given consciously or mechanically. The body is endowed with beauty and youth when it is under the direction of positive ideas. In layman's terms, we may say that those with good emotional health and acute awareness of their thoughts, behaviors, and feelings are the ones who have mastered coping mechanisms for stress, anxiety, and other common problems that come with daily life.

The body will quickly degenerate and become infected with illnesses and anxiety if you poison it with negative thoughts, though.

When the body is ill, negative thoughts that are deeply ingrained and mental in origin become quite evident. Negative thoughts have been shown to injure the body, and they have even been found to hasten a man's death. People who frequently experience negative thoughts are people who live in fear.

The body is greatly demoralized by anxiety, which makes the body and mind vulnerable to illness. Your blood will continue to be immoral and poisoned if you keep spreading evil thoughts. It's like putting filthy hen in socks if you don't alter your perspective. The alteration in nutrition, however, will only be one ingredient once your thoughts are clear. Positive thoughts lead to positive behaviors. On the other side, the same is true. So protecting your mind is just as vital as perfecting your physique. Unfortunately, the majority of people have thoughts of envy, disillusionment, malice, and hopelessness that undermine their physical well-being and beauty.

Emotional control can only be improved if you are aware of your feelings and know how to manage them. You should also be aware of what's causing your stress, unhappiness, and anxiety. You can preserve your emotional well-being in this manner. One strategy to manage your emotions is to lead a balanced life. In today's fast-paced world, many activities—such as schoolwork and workplace issues—can cause us to feel bad.

Even if you put on a smiling face, you may feel apprehensive, stressed, or upset. Even while it is a good idea to deal with these unpleasant emotions, you should instead concentrate on the good things in your life. You must also let go of those aspects of your life that overwhelm and stress you.

To restore emotional equilibrium, calm your mind and body using techniques like meditation. We also found that those who live in dread are the ones who are most impacted by unfavorable ideas.

Therefore, it is essential to build resilience. Resilient people stand a higher chance of managing stress healthily. However, you should be able to express yourself because making positive changes can be just as hard as quitting unhealthy habits.

For the law of attraction to work for you, there are some things you may do and should avoid. When contemplating the workings of the cosmos, it is simple to become overburdened by its complexity. The universe has already taught you that sometimes it's just as vital to know what to do as it is to know what not to do.

Your success won't necessarily be prevented by your mistakes; some will only slow it down, while others may completely stop it. Regardless, recognizing what you are doing incorrectly is the only way for you to correct it, and every mistake has a fix. Time is the one that most people have trouble with both in general and in terms of the answer; they assume that everything will happen instantly or at least quickly. The universe is an exception to that rule. You must give yourself time to identify the issue as well as time to determine whether the proposed solution is effective. Things will change, so have some patience with yourself and the universe.

Avoid common errors by:

Instantaneous satisfaction

We all want things to happen quickly since, after all, we live in a fast-paced world.

But we discovered that the universe has a gestation time and functions accordingly. Despite this, a lot of people desire it presently. The seeds you plant with your ideas and feelings will eventually bloom, just like a flower must. You must make time for your goals and stick to the road that has been laid out for you. The future will change, so don't set impractical deadlines; instead, rejoice and express gratitude for the present. This will take time.

Attached

The universe functions differently from how we do; it works with vibrations and energies. Try to avoid becoming emotionally invested in a certain result inslead, and just concentrate on the feelings it will bring you instead, as the universe will provide those. So, be thankful even if your ideal career or vehicle falls short of your expectations but still brings you the same level of satisfaction. In the end, even if the image is not what you had imagined, it is the feelings that matter and is most significant.

Decided Route

We are guilty of this because we plan the route that will get us there in addition to visualizing our destination. Some are more thorough than others; some refer to it as their "five-year plan," etc. Because things fluctuate, the law of attraction and the cosmos do not deal with preconceived plans. Therefore, if you are one of the people who have their life planned out but still want to employ the law of attraction, you may need to be ready to let your plan change significantly or disappear entirely. Because the universe is so preoccupied with the now and now, rather than the here and now in five years, it is likely that your journey will diverge from the one you had planned.

Sometimes people try it, decide it doesn't work for them, which is untrue because it always works whether we want it to or not, and give up for one of the aforementioned reasons. As a result, if you are having issues or doubts, have a look at these common errors and make modifications as necessary.

Too Much

Because people frequently start big, this connects to the first error.

Even if the law of attraction applies equally whether you're trying to manifest a new set of shoes or a new home, the universe understands what you're doing. The fact that these two things signify different things to you, though, is what counts. That doesn't mean you shouldn't try to manifest your ideal home; it just means that it takes time for the law of attraction to completely sink into your mind and that until then, it won't function as intended. Start with something that will enable you to strengthen that idea so that you are completely convinced it is true—after all, your prior experiences are evidence that it is.

Desperation

From a pit of despair, we frequently express our needs and wants. We hear ourselves saying things like, "I need to get a lover," or "I need to get a better career." Statements like these are not spoken from a place of joy, but rather out of a desperate attempt to get out of the hole we believe we are in. First of all, this indicates that you cannot be happy without someone else and that you can never be happy if you do not get another employment. Your restricting and unfavorable beliefs will be entangled with your other emotions, which will send conflicting messages to the universe. Decide on things that will easily boost and maintain your happiness instead of concentrating on what makes you unhappy.

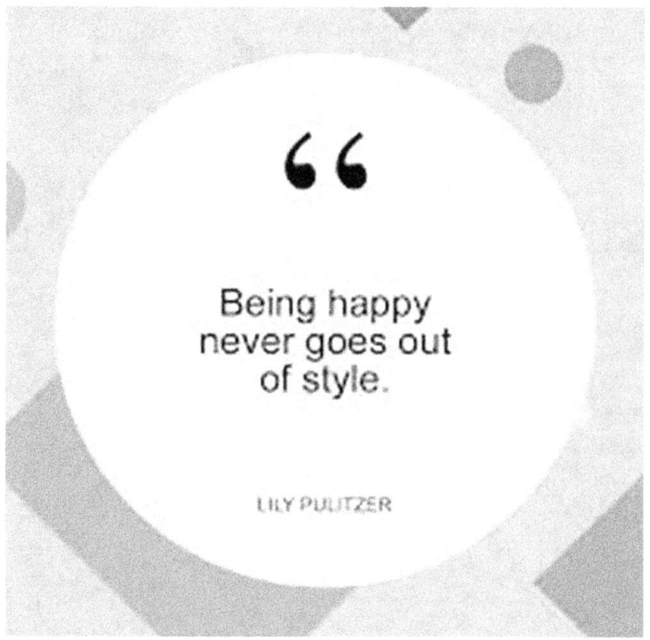

Phony Gratitude

Gratitude is the cornerstone of the law of attraction because like attracts like.

Although some people need a little more mental adjustment than others in this area, the bottom line is the same: if you are not sincere in your gratitude for what you have, you will discover that the universe is less kind. This is because the cosmos is merely mirroring what your thoughts and emotions are projecting out into the universe. Investigate the aspects of your life for which you are genuinely grateful, and then celebrate them. Focus on the feelings that come over you as you consider all that you have to be thankful for both in the morning and before you go to sleep.

Positive Mentality

Because they believe all they need to do is think happy thoughts, people frequently give up on the law of attraction.

Thoughts alone are not enough to solve problems, though. We must deliberately and consistently develop our positive mental muscles because our brains naturally preferentially scan and remember negative memories.

The internal landscape of our thoughts has been created by a variety of anxieties, obstacles, myths, and limiting beliefs that we all frequently hold. Positive thinking alone cannot fix any of these problems overnight.

The patterns that have been formed and stored in our unconscious must be changed, then they must be replaced with empowered, positive patterns to manifest using the law of attraction. You are gaining knowledge on brain rewiring. You must add constructive habits into your everyday routines to properly accomplish this; this will elevate and shift your energetic frequency. To manifest from a peaceful place where the action will be encouraged and results will come more quickly, it is necessary to change your energetic vibration. You will lay the groundwork for positive outcomes and experiences by using strategies that introduce these fresh, constructive thoughts into your mind.

Excellent Daily Habits Move:

On a molecular level, our bodies also store negative emotions. Moving around is one of the finest methods to relieve stress and purge the body of bad energy. Walking, yoga and dancing are all effective alternatives to strenuous exercise if you don't want to.

Find a regimen that motivates you to get up and move around; just make sure it works for you.

Journal of gratitude Experiencing thankfulness is among the simplest methods to boost our energy. You will naturally be in a good mood and your energetic vibration will rise if you appreciate everything you have and acknowledge your blessings.

Anxiety List: It seems sensible that we worry so much given that the brain retains unfavorable memories. It's merely the brain's natural tendency to do that. Keep a concern list for two weeks and add to it whenever you find yourself worrying. Everything you worry about should be on your list, from major, enduring concerns to minor, passing problems. If you worry about it, put it on paper.

Keep a list with you at all times so you can easily jot down important details. You might be surprised at how much time is spent fretting. The heavy energy that holds us stuck can be released through this practice, and after the two weeks are through, you'll realize that your anxieties weren't necessary. Your brain will see the list as evidence that worrying is fruitless and a waste of time.

A deep breath: Practice deep breathing that originates from the belly, rather than breathing shallowly or from the chest.

This method of breathing activates the parasympathetic nervous system, which is known to contribute to a feeling of peace and contentment within the body. This prepares us to act with inspiration from a position of clarity and calmness, which improves our chances of success.

Focus: It's crucial to begin paying attention to what you concentrate on throughout the day.

Do you focus more on what is going well or wrong when things are going poorly? When you are trying to manifest your dreams, challenges and other barriers will unavoidably arise. However, focusing on what is right can help you develop the skills necessary to overcome problems effectively, which will boost your self-assurance and raise your energy vibration. By doing this, you'll be able to overcome and get beyond challenges more quickly.

Meditation is particularly beneficial for people with overactive minds because they tend to be more pessimistic. Although meditation does not prevent you from thinking, it does assist to reduce the power that thoughts have over us and calming even the most overactive minds. This will eventually divert attention away from the unfavorable and demanding routines we have developed throughout our lives.

Visualize: One way to enter your subconscious mind is to replace the negative thought patterns that our brains frequently produce with new, positive ones. Make sure to read your list both before you fall asleep at night and in the morning. Spend around five minutes reflecting on the emotion you get when you accomplish your goals rather than simply reading it and moving on with your day. You should keep in mind that connecting to the sense of success as well as the image is what we need to do.

Make a list of your goals to get started on the path of inspired action. This is another writing

exercise. A list will help you connect to the "why" behind each goal and will provide you with clarity. This is important because it will help you connect your "why" to how it will feel to accomplish your objective. By successfully establishing a connection to this emotion, you may elevate your vibration and attract the situations and people that will support your goals.

Pretend: Think about how it was to be a child when nothing was impractical when it came to pursuing your ambitions. It may seem strange to try to feel as though you already have what you want when you don't, so practicing this step is necessary. While doing this, you'll feel joyful and eager, which will raise your vibration.

While doing all of these tasks every day is not required, the more you can accomplish the better. Although it requires time and persistence, brain retraining is worthwhile in the long run. To materialize your desires in the future, the best method to boost your vibration is to feel content, liberated, and stable in the here and now.

The law of attraction's core tenet is that you attract what you give energy to. If you spend your days fretting about your finances and increasing bills, you can't help but feel uneasy and unfavorable, which only serves to attract more unfavorable people. If you do not feel the freedom, security, and joy that you desire, no matter how hard you try to think positively and how many times you repeat affirmations throughout the day, your manifestations will continue to elude you.

Although like attracts like, this does not imply that your goals and ideas will draw in material things. The thing that attracts is how you feel. In essence, the thing that is ordering something from the cosmos is your feeling. If you want to make more money yet feel anxious and lacking, you will just attract more tension and lack. You will draw in more of what you don't want rather than getting what you desire.

The following two steps will assist you in changing your feelings:

Develop Possibilities

The chance to mend will present itself once you have identified the unfavorable thoughts that fuel your vicious cycle. You can achieve this by examining and analyzing your thoughts, which will open up a wider range of options than just the unfavorable ones that would have previously been your default. Sometimes we can't help it, and we frequently cause ourselves stress by imagining the worst-case situation. You won't be able to escape your rut if you keep believing that the worst-case scenario is the only one that could happen.

The greatest and simplest way to deal with this is to imagine other scenarios that might result in a more comfortable outcome. Even if you don't believe that everything will work out perfectly, even just believing that things are getting easier will give you a vital sense of optimism and joy. It is crucial to keep in mind that even the most complex issues can be solved in a variety of ways. So it will be much more beneficial to think about alternative options rather than going to the worst-case scenario.

Source: You should be aware that every feeling you experience is the result of thinking. For instance, if you get a bill in the mail, you might worry that you'll have to ask your family for a loan or that you'll lose your automobile. These ideas could make you feel anxious or afraid. It's critical to identify the specific thoughts that are making you feel bad.

This is crucial because if you don't figure out what thoughts are triggering the sentiments, you'll keep having these negative thoughts, which will inevitably lead to negative sensations. Only by breaking the cycle can you be successful. This can be intimidating, but if you start to identify the thoughts that are making you feel this way, you will be able to stop them from recurring in the future.

Affirmations Have Power

Affirmations have a powerful creative force and a certain vibratory frequency that decides whether you will attract the things you desire to attract, even though they may appear to be meaningless words. Affirmations are typically stated in certain situations, but you don't have to say them in certain situations for them to be helpful. Keep in mind that you attract whatever is in a given vibratory zone more while you are in it. In this situation, it is simpler for whatever you want to happen to manifest right away when your thoughts are preoccupied with your affirmations or when you speak the things that you want to see in your life.

When you repeatedly say your affirmations, you will begin to live the future you want for yourself. Although you can write these affirmations down in a journal, it's important to have the right mindset about how to come up with effective affirmations for various circumstances if you want to close the vibrational gap between your current vibrational frequency and the vibrational frequency you must be in to manifest your goals.

Here are some guidelines to remember when coming up with affirmations for any area of your life:

Never include negatives in your affirmations; always be positive.

Don't add prohibitions to your affirmations. For instance, instead of saying "I don't want to be impoverished," say "The cosmos is full of wealth for me to tap." Even if you don't want something, believing that you just don't want it and want anything else won't change your circumstances. If you include don'ts in your affirmations that pertain to your finances, you will draw poverty your way. You probably already know that the things you fear the most in life are usually the ones that happen to you.

For instance, even if you repeatedly tell yourself that you don't want negative nightmares, you will almost certainly experience them. If something is on your mind, you will draw it; the universe doesn't distinguish between what you want and what you don't!

You might attract poverty even though you haven't recently given much thought to it. This may occur if you were thinking about poverty at a time when it was taking up a significant portion of your subconscious mind and it was still close to the vibrational frequency you were in.

Your subconscious mind functions like a radio, broadcasting to the universe all of your thoughts, feelings, anxieties, perceptions, likes, and wishes. Remember that when your subconscious mind has some reservations about your ability to generate the life you want, you cannot trick yourself into believing affirmations. Even if you haven't lately vibrated the wrong kind of energy, those subconscious doubts are what send vibrational echoes back to plague you.

You must avoid the recurrent thoughts and behaviors that force you to return to your skeptical self and attract negative energy, which manifests as unfavorable outcomes in your life if you want your dreams to materialize right away.

Keep your declarations Affirmative

Simply affirming is insufficient to help you start living the life you want to live; you also need to keep your affirmations powerful and inspiring. For instance, your affirmations shouldn't only express your desire for a manifestation; instead, they should be strong enough to convey your manifestation. It will be simpler for you to enter the vibratory zone of your ideal life the more your subconscious mind believes it. In other words, you're tricking yourself into thinking that your desires have already come to pass.

By doing so, you begin to live in the vibratory range of the things you desire to materialize in your life, which makes it easier for them to do so. In reality, like always attracts like, therefore the more you believe that something has occurred in your life, the easier it will be for you to attract it.

Keep Your Affirmations Vibrationally Close at Hand

You don't want to put yourself in a position to become frustrated or negative, which would start a cycle of uncertainty and disappointment. If you want any of your affirmations to manifest right away, make sure they are inside or close to your frequency range to avoid manifesting difficulties. Your amount of belief will depend on how challenging a situation you see for your manifestations to occur.

Being honest with yourself about this can help you get to the point where you can honestly say that you believe there are endless possibilities. At that point, you can start saying affirmations that are completely beyond your vibrational range and still expect them to come true.

How to Manifest All Your Affirmations Immediately

Creating potent affirmations is far from sufficient to bring about the required manifestations immediately. If you want to reduce the difficulty of manifesting anything in your life, you need to be correctly connected with the things you wish to attract. You will then experience instant manifestations of everything you desire in your life as a result. How do you then get to the point where you are ready to draw in whatever it is that you want to materialize in your life?

Alter or control your thought patterns.

The driving factor behind what people draw to themselves is thought. To start believing with complete honesty that what you affirm will appear in your life, it is crucial to prepare yourself to the point where you can control your thoughts. For instance, if you want to recover from a condition, stop thinking like a patient and start acting and thinking like someone who has recovered. Your health will instantly manifest as a result of this drawing vibration that you would experience if you were healthy. You can achieve an optimum vibrational balance that will continuously enable you to effortlessly materialize everything you want in your life the more thought balance you can master.

Be Clear About What You Want.

No matter what it is, something will be drawn to you by your vibes. Have a goal in mind that you want to see come to pass in your life rather than expecting the universe to just provide it to you. Affirm the amount of compensation you want to receive if you seek a raise. Similar to this, if you wish to win the lotto, be specific and specify how much you hope to win. You can only do this to begin vibrating at the frequency of the manifestations you wish to see in your life.

Give the universe no rules.

As much as you should be precise about the things you want to happen in your life right away, try not to be too picky and precise about the exact way you want your affirmations to come true. You should have faith that the universe pays attention to your regular affirmations in life. You'll begin to doubt your ability to attract what you want as you focus more on the how a portion of the attraction. Once you have declared what you want, let your unlimited vibrations take control and let the universe handle the rest.

The next step is to just sit back and wait for your manifestation to come true.

It's time to take a closer look at how you can use the Law of Attraction to your advantage and bring about the positive manifestations you desire in your life now that you have a better understanding of the fundamentals of the Law of Attraction and a list of 100 potent affirmations to use in a variety of situations. You should examine every aspect of your life and identify any locations that produce unfavorable vibrations because you should stay away from them. You must go forward and adopt a new viewpoint to apply the Law of Attraction and everything that it entails.

Despite how dreadful a situation may seem, it always has positive sides, therefore you must seek them out. Everything is entirely up to you, and everyone has the same options. Never assume that others had a greater chance of happiness and fulfillment at birth than you did. Do you believe that being wealthy equates to being content?

It doesn't matter what you own. It doesn't matter what you have. It has to do with how you feel on the inside and what you draw into your life. It is what everyone needs to comprehend. To manifest exactly what you believe you need in life, learn to let go of negative thoughts and project good energy.

Dreams and Setting Goals

The definition of what is important for you right now is the only urgent thing.

Everyone successful follows the same formula, whether they are aware of it or not.

- It only takes four simple steps. but strong.

- They are the secret to all success.

- We present to you:

The unbeatable recipe for achievement

1. Be very clear about what you want. You must be quite precise.
2. Take immediate action. It is insufficient to merely wish.
3. Examine what functions and what doesn't. Avoid wasting time and effort on futile strategies.
4. Alter your behavior as often as necessary to achieve your goals. Your ability to adapt your course of action will let you try new things until you achieve success.

Never postpone experiencing joy.

Most people put off tackling their goals until after they have committed themselves to live their lives to the fullest.

Success, like being allowed to be happy, differs greatly from the enjoyment we have when taking the necessary steps to achieve success.

Live each day to the fullest and savor every happy moment that comes your way.

Instead of viewing your life as the journey you must take before achieving a goal, take it as a pleasure and keep in mind that your personal development is far more significant than any imperfect achievements you may achieve.

- Where are you heading at the moment?

- Are you advancing toward or away from your objectives?

- Do you need to alter your practices?

As you work toward your objectives, do you like your life? If not, immediately alter your attitude in the relevant area. Save your time.

Spend a moment appreciating all you have now that was once just a wish by thinking about it.

Although there were undoubtedly many challenges on the way to getting there, it is already a regular part of your life today.

Remember that you have already faced similar challenges and prevailed whenever you doubt your abilities to realize your dreams.

Your motivation and strong will make you unstoppable.

Only when you are completely certain of what you want and when you are certain that no obstacle can stop you from achieving it will the unstoppable desire to win manifest.

The influence of goals

"Any path leaves you fine when you don't know where you want to go," the saying goes.

Your life will swing back and forth, with frequent ups and downs, if your objectives are not clear.

The ability to constantly know where one is going is one of the key traits of successful people. They promptly alter their course of action to proceed directly in the direction of their goal because they have an accurate understanding of whether they are veering away from it.

With the help of this straightforward seven-step process, we can identify objectives that properly match our future vision.

Step 1: Choose a goal.

Asking yourself this question will help.

Pick a target. Then several. Do they have any similarities?

For instance, motivation is a factor in your ability to organize your workplace, begin a diet, and complete tasks you begin.

As a result, the common factor among them all is the capacity for motivation.

To accurately define your goals, make sure to analyze every one of them.

A Check

Make sure your objective is stated in terms of what you desire, not what you do not.

For instance, "I don't want to eat so much between meals," "I don't want to feel like a failure," and "I want to quit procrastinating." All of these words are used in the context of what we don't desire.

We may simply change them into what we want: "I want to act right now and solve the problem," "I want to feel good about myself," and "I want to eat fruits and vegetables in between meals."

By making their unconscious creative mind concentrate on what they don't want or wish to avoid, people wind up manifesting such things in their lives.

Your route to success will fundamentally change once you start thinking about what you desire.

B Check

Make sure your objective is stated so that, regardless of what others do, you will accomplish it.

Setting goals that depend on other people changing, making specific decisions, or thinking of an event for our benefit is a mistake.

We must focus our changes on ourselves; it is incorrect to focus them on others.

The incorrect objective, for instance, is "I want other people to quit criticizing me."

It calls for us to exert control over other people's behavior and free choice.

Since we are making a change that is centered on ourselves, the statement "I want to have a high self-esteem and feel optimistic even if I am criticized" is appropriate.

Step 2: Post a "goal sign" there.

How will you know when you've accomplished your objective?

Many people struggle to find a signal that tells them when they've accomplished something, which hinders them from feeling content and satisfied when they do.

As a result, they are unable to determine if their everyday actions are bringing them closer or further away from their objectives.

For instance, if my objective is to "be successful," and success is not precisely defined, it is feasible that I will achieve many things and even raise my level of living, but I will not be able to document this improvement.

Success can be defined as the publication of a book, winning a loved one, or making $10,000.

What matters is who sets the objective. It needs to be distinctly specified in any instance.

Check

Is there a connection between the goal and the goal sign?

The goal signal you choose must give you precise and accurate information about your success.

For instance, I would be making a mistake if my objective was to improve my sales skills and my signal was how I felt at the end of the day. Although feeling satisfied is good, it does not necessarily indicate that my sales abilities are increasing.

The number of orders I've received and the quantity of commission money I've made might be a more realistic indicator.

As another illustration, let's say that I want to "be a competent and sympathetic parent." Again, if my indicator is how often my kids compliment me, then I am in error.

A better clue would be to monitor how my children act in everyday life and if they inform me about their troubles when they need advice.

step 3.

Choose the location, timing, and people you wish to work with in

For our subconscious creative mind to produce the right results, it is crucial to pinpoint these checkpoints precisely.

There are actual reference data that turns into daydreams when our aims are not grounded.

Fixing the precise location enables us to pinpoint the physical reality of our surroundings. Would you be willing to give up all you hold dear and move to an Arab emirate to live, for instance, if our goal is "to make ten thousand dollars a month"?

Regarding the following question, is it possible for you to accomplish that aim in six months as it is in six years?

And finally, do you care if you accomplish that objective all by yourself or if you share it with others?

Our goals must be precisely stated to produce fully defined indications that will allow the Law of Attraction to function as intended.

Check

It must be quite detailed. What signs will you pick up on, hear, or experience that will indicate you've succeeded in your mission?

To ensure that your goal is precise, including the three points that we investigate in this stage.

Step 4: Examine the barriers.

What is preventing you from achieving your objective right now, you might ask yourself?

If nothing comes to mind, move on to the next stage without wasting any time.

However, the primary purpose frequently clashes with other objectives.

If this is the case, it is crucial to figure out how to accomplish both objectives in unison. In general, if we shift our emphasis, competing goals tend to reinforce one another.

If they can't be united, they can be programmed to synchronize to avoid colliding with one another.

Let's use a real-world illustration. Let's use the objective we established in the preceding step—"earn $10,000 every month"—as a guide. I can tackle this issue in the two methods mentioned above if, after asking myself the question, it becomes apparent that I lack the personal traits necessary to reach that figure.

The first would be to put effort into cultivating those traits as I work on my primary objective.

The alternative would be to give those traits my complete attention first and only then turn my full concentration to achieving my financial goal.

Find the materials you already have in Step 5

Ask yourself: What tools do I already have at my disposal that will enable me to accomplish my objective?

What elements of your aim, such as being able to talk clearly in front of an audience, can you already achieve?

You might already be able to talk, stand up, face the audience in the eye, use humor to communicate yourself, dress elegantly, etc.

Therefore, it's critical to evaluate and adequately value the resources we already have.

Expand your resources in step 6

Ask yourself this question: What resources could you add to help you reach your goal?

You must think about the components you need to complete your goal. Like, for instance, if you need to learn anything, look for resources, speak with experts in the field, etc. Of course, you also need to have the self-confidence to take on and complete what you propose. Are you self-assured enough to use the Law of Attraction to follow your objective?

Plan in Step 7

How am I going to achieve my goal, ask yourself. What should I do first, exactly?

You should keep in mind that while certain goals will be accomplished quickly, others may take longer to complete owing to their complexity. As a result, we need strong targets to drive us ahead, but we also need to set smaller goals to act as intermediate milestones on the way to our ultimate goal.

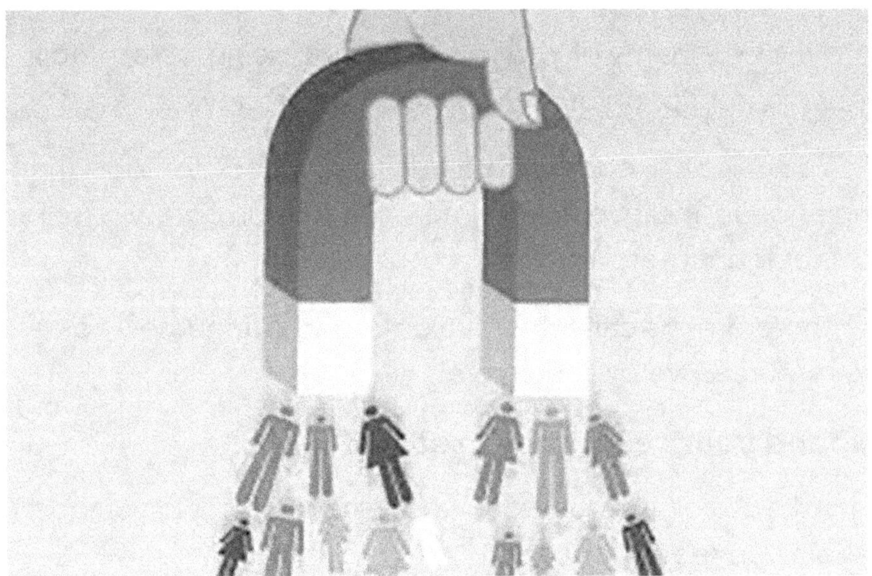

The Influence of Vision

Do you recall the words that Lewis Carroll's Cheshire Cat used in Alice in Wonderland? "It doesn't matter which way you go if you don't know where you are going." You must be very clear in your mind about what you want and where you need to go. Only then does the paradigm change, bringing about a new reality for you. Imagine having your ideal career, new home, stable relationship with your partner, or new vehicle. We all have countless wants and desires. You can want something as long as it serves a purpose.

You can use the Law of Attraction to achieve goals by using visualization.

Your ability to concentrate and experience your vision as if it were already real can help. This will compel you much more to take action and achieve your objective. You will acquire momentum by taking these steps, and before you know it, your goals will be within reach. Through visualization, you may sharpen your attention and redirect the fear and procrastination that are holding you back from attaining your goals.

Start by soothing your body and mind to improve your ability to concentrate. This will enable you to discover your authentic self.

You will have access to the universe's limitless supply of energy. You can get rid of all the bad thoughts and change your energy to radiate positive vibrations when your mind is calm. The Law of Attraction might present you with possibilities, but to achieve your goals, you must take advantage of those opportunities. The Universe will respond to the correct opportunities, through cause and effect, to help you reach your goals more quickly when you cooperate with it to do so.

"You create your thoughts, your thoughts generate your intentions, and your intentions build your reality," as Wayne Dyer once remarked. You must devote all of your attention to your creation. As if it were your reality, live it. When you do this, you will radiate good energy into the universe, and it will recognize that you are serious. You will receive opportunities to realize your dreams in response to it. Maintain a connection to your dream. Sense it.

Enjoy the journey and feel satisfied with it. Your focus will increase as a result, and your vibrational energy will be strengthened. Give it love and thank the universe for giving it to you. Love, goodness, and gratitude are what the Universe is made of. Being grateful for your new circumstances can help you draw abundance from the universe. From this point forward, let the Universe assist you as you enjoy the journey! Make sure you don't have any negative thoughts when you're concentrating on your goals because they could interfere with your energy for manifestation and prevent you from achieving your goals.

You can use the power of imagination to bring your goals to life by following the five easy steps stated below:

Clearly state and be very explicit about your goals. Your genuine aims and intentions must be crystal clear in your mind. Be very detailed. Consider your motivations for your desires and the role they will play in your life. Will pursuing your goals make you happy?

A clear vision of your goals will make them easier to achieve and manifest more quickly. You need focus and tenacity to accomplish your goals. Try to relax your body and mind to better grasp your demands.

Make a connection to your inner self, and let your inner energy and intuition help you make judgments.

Get rid of mental clutter so that the universe can fulfill your actual desires. You'll be able to hear the vibrations coming from the universe once you can achieve a deep level of relaxation. This will enable you to focus on your desires and select the options that are ideal for you. Make sure to visualize what you truly want, not what someone else wants for you, as Jerry Gillies advised.

Now is the time to ignite your ambitions by using all of your confidence and tenacity. Shift your energy and concentrate your emotions on your goals. Negativity should not exist because it can prevent your manifestation. Maintain a positive outlook in your head and embrace it. Your ability to spread happy vibrations to the universe increases with your level of positivity. Your chances of success will soar when you are composed, at ease, and concentrated. While you concentrate on visualization, your default state should be relaxation.

Only a persistent imagination and an attitude of gratitude can give you the chance to experience sweet success.

Constantly visualize your goals. Your motivation to start working toward your goals will increase if you consistently visualize them in your mind. You must put forth the effort to use the Law of Attraction to bring your dreams to pass. Keep in mind that you can design your reality. Remember to remain composed and concentrated. According to Jim Carrey, "I would picture things coming to me. It would only improve my mood. If you put in the effort, visualization works. That is the issue.

You can't merely picture something and eat a sandwich. We all know that before beginning his acting career, Jim Carrey traveled along Mulholland Drive in Los Angeles. He would picture himself collaborating with renowned producers and directors. He pictured himself as an actress earning millions of dollars. His perseverance paid off, and he has established himself as a successful, accomplished actor who is paid very well.

Establish a concrete plan to accomplish your objectives

You must establish a specific plan to attain the desired outcomes. You are utterly mistaken if you believe that you can fulfill your wishes simply by visualizing them. No genie with a magic lamp is standing by to hear your requests and promptly fulfill them.

The universe's laws can be used to speed up the process, but you still need to be persistent and committed to your goal. If you desire something passionately enough, you may encounter obstacles along the way, but you cannot give up. The Universe will cooperate with you to assist create opportunities if you work diligently toward your goals. You must take advantage of these chances to get where you're going. You can use the rich supply of energy within you to assist you in reaching your objectives if you maintain a peaceful and relaxed state of mind.

Adjust as you go - Take a stop and unwind if you encounter difficulties along the route or feel that something is not functioning properly. Identify your authentic self. The universe will provide the answers for you. You'll discover answers to your difficulties. Return to your original issue and continue to fight until you reach your goal.

To bring anything into your life, assume that it already exists, as Richard Back once stated. Anyone may achieve their goals and enjoy a prosperous life, whether it is in their profession or in interpersonal connections. They only have to give it a go! If you have a lack of abundance mindset, you will undermine your energy for manifestation and experience nothing but failure and hopelessness throughout your entire life. It's time to make changes in your life and discover your goals. What then prevents you from achieving your goals?

Mind-Over-Matter Techniques

Perhaps the best thing you could ever do is nothing.

The primary goal of traditional meditation is to destroy and let go of false beliefs that keep reality from affecting your daily life.

Because of everyone's increasing stress levels from working long hours for little pay and the diseases that seem to be getting worse in our supposedly "modern civilization," meditation is becoming more and more popular around our globe. The general public is being introduced to meditation as a way to unwind, yet that is merely a side effect.

The first gateway medication that widens and opens the human mind to altered states of consciousness is meditation. It can help you connect with long-forgotten memories, spiritual encounters, lost items, and loved ones who have departed, read people's minds, communicate with angels or guides, and learn the real meaning of who you are as a person. There are a ton of different techniques to meditate, but only four will help you expand your business.

The first type of meditation involves visualizing your primary objectives.

Entering a new paradigm is the key to doing so. Focusing on the present only causes it to be repeated in the future if you are unhappy with some aspect of your current reality. Your prior thoughts contributed to the creation of everything in your life as it is today.

Therefore, every thinking you have right now will influence how you live in the future.

Keep in mind that the actions you take will reflect the perspective and values you hold. Regularly thinking new thoughts will alter your perspective and have a cascading influence on your reality.

To live a happy life or to make a portion of your life happier, you must first learn to develop a new habit of thinking of your life as you want it to be. This is known as creating a new reality or a new paradigm. You must develop a clear picture of the life you want, think creatively, and consider it from several perspectives. You have your vision when you develop your key aim. Correct the details, then take action by recording them all.

Spend 10 to 15 minutes per day reflecting on it. Think about the vision and picture of what would happen if it were already happening in the present. Put your eyes closed and become lost in it. Feel it physically, emotionally, and olfactorily. Engage all of your senses as much as you can by hearing people speak to you and offering you congratulations.

Feel the ocean waves rock the yacht you are on while holding the cheque in your hand. Imagine yourself experiencing the scene as it is happening right now. You are bringing your desire into the present via what you are doing.

You exert more effort into anything the more often you do it. the more strongly you are drawn to that frequency. As a result, the more charge it contains, the more ripples it will cause in your vibration. When you're through, give yourself and everyone in your immediate vicinity a heartfelt thank you for your vision. You will eventually experience the same thing or something better.

Replay a portion of your vision in your head as you go about your day as if it were a pleasant memory. Feel the want to be in the now.

This is how the power of thought over matter is enforced. Instead of responding to the present as it is and seeing it, bring your desire into the moment and impose your vision as if it were real. This is what it feels like to be a visionary—to overlay your vision over the world as it is right now.

It could be challenging to accomplish this while going about your daily activities, particularly when talking to other people. It's advisable to at least start modest and build your way up; speaking with confidence is crucial. if you want 40 clients but only see 5–10 per week. If you can get the confidence to answer 40 when someone asks how many clients you see each week, do so.

If not, start modestly, perhaps with 15-20. As you gain those 15-20 over time and engage in interactions with others, the number will steadily increase. Think carefully before you speak. It is preferable to be quiet than to say something that might undermine your efforts.

We must purposefully create our desires through the human interface with reality to avoid repeating the past that we want to move on from. So many people are trained to just talk about their past. Unless it was a nice past—which, for the majority of us, it wasn't—we must stop doing that. We must develop a vision, hone it as needed, speak as much as we can about it, concentrate on it every day, and keep it at the forefront of our minds.

The future is determined by the here and now. Use it sensibly.

How to Improve Concentration and Attention

Increasing your focus can help you in a variety of ways other than the Law of Attraction. Have you ever had trouble overcoming a hurdle, preparing for a big exam, or even finishing a tricky project? If so, you might have wished you could have improved your ability to focus. Think of focus as nothing more than the mental effort you are doing to complete the activity or learn the material you are now dealing with. Contrast this with your attention span, which is only the amount of time you can devote to focusing on a single task or area of study.

Our ability to focus is influenced by a variety of events, and both our attention span and concentration are susceptible to disruption. True, some people find it difficult to just ignore distractions.

Some people also think that becoming older and not getting enough sleep can make it difficult to focus.

There is evidence to suggest that as we get older, forgetting things becomes simpler, and when memory loss is present, our attention suffers. Additionally, any physical wounds like a head concussion or brain injuries may impair our ability to focus. Even more so, a variety of mental health issues also affect our capacity for concentration.

It is normal to feel frustrated when trying to focus yet failing. This frequently results in annoyance and stress, which makes it much harder to concentrate on the goal of learning. If any of this rings a bell, you may benefit from using these scientifically proven techniques to sharpen your focus.

Train your brain as our first piece of advice. It doesn't happen very often when you think of playing games to get better at something.

You can improve your focus and concentration by playing games that require concentration. Games like Sudoku, Sudoki, Memory Games, Chess, Crossword Puzzles, Jigsaw Puzzles, and Word Searches or Scrabbles

Spending roughly 15 minutes a day, five days a week, on brain-training exercises can have a significant influence on concentration and focus, according to a study of 4,715 adults.

Additionally, playing brain-training games strengthens your short-term memory and enhances your ability to solve problems.

Adults shouldn't be the only ones who can focus and concentrate.

Children can get the same results. We should involve our kids in improving their concentration and focus as well as teaching them about the Law of Attraction and how to produce the good things in their lives. These abilities last a lifetime. As noted previously, we discover that a similar mechanism happens in kids when they play games.

Additionally, several studies have found that coloring might be advantageous for both kids and adults. More focus and concentration are required as we move toward a more detailed hue, which in turn works your brain.

The benefits of brain games on mental exercise are even more significant for older persons. Considering that memory and focus get worse with aging. 2,842 persons were assessed for the study, and then those same adults were contacted again ten years later. In the beginning, memory, cognition, and processing abilities were enhanced in individuals who used cognitive training for 10 to 14 sessions. The participants said their capacity for carrying out daily tasks had not decreased since the trial's start, and some even said it had improved, when they were checked on ten years later.

Consider stepping outside of your comfort zone and playing video games as the second piece of advice. According to recent studies, playing video games may improve attentiveness. In a 2018 study with 29 participants, there was evidence to support the idea that playing video games for an hour can enhance our visual selective attention.

This is our capacity to pay attention to one thing while ignoring distractions.

Another study from 2017 discovered evidence to imply that playing video games causes changes in the brain, including improvements in attention and focus, after reviewing a variety of information.

Improved sleep is our next piece of advice. Lack of sleep can interfere with a variety of bodily processes, including your capacity for concentration and attention. Yes, the odd sleepless night might not have a big impact on you. However, skipping out on regular rest might impact your mood as well as how well you perform at work.

Lack of sleep does not only have an impact on these regions; it can also impair reflexes, making it difficult to perform daily activities like driving.

Those who struggle to obtain adequate sleep frequently do so because of their health, their busy schedules, or other considerations.

But it's important to obtain the necessary amount of sleep as frequently as you can. Experts recommend that adults sleep for approximately 7 to 8 hours per night. Here are some suggestions for bettering sleep quality and hastening sleep.

- Working out three to five days a week for 15 to 20 minutes.

- But stay away from strenuous exercise right before night.

- Establish a schedule and wake up at roughly the same time every day, including on weekends and days off.

- The environment should be cool but inviting.

- Switch off all electronics—including the TV—at least one hour before going to bed.

- The fourth tip is to schedule regular exercise. Many people discover a link between better concentration and frequent exercise.

A 2018 research of 116 fifth graders revealed that after just four weeks, those who engaged in daily physical activity had improved focus and attention. Additionally, research has shown that older persons who engage in some form of physical activity may be able to slow memory loss and improve focus.

There are other methods to fit exercise into your day if you belong to a group that struggles to find the time or if you don't want to join a gym. Your heart rate should increase while you work out. So, here are some suggestions for incorporating fitness into your day.

- Every morning, get up 20 minutes early and jog or walk around your neighborhood.

- Break up your weekly grocery runs into many visits, and park toward the back of the lot.

- Just like you would for a meeting, set aside time to exercise.

- Exercise during lunch.

- Keep moving. Perform toe raises, squats, or lunges while you wait for the subway or microwave to finish cooking.

Quit being a slacker; nothing requires you to only sit and watch TV. While you're being amused, use this time to exercise. You can use a treadmill to walk, jump rope, or perform any other workouts that are suitable for your level of fitness.

A brief bout of exercise before you need to concentrate on a task can also assist you to boost focus, according to some research.

Fifth advice: go outside. Get outside every day if you want to improve both your ability to focus and your sense of connection to the environment. You may sit in your backyard or take a quick stroll through the park, even if it's only for 15 to 20 minutes. There are several advantages to allowing yourself to be in a natural setting. There are favorable effects on the natural environment, according to research.

According to a 2014 study, having plants around the office can improve focus, concentration, and productivity as well as workplace satisfaction and air quality. Think about putting a few plants in your house or office to assist you to create a more natural atmosphere. Succulents are a great option for low-maintenance plants that don't require a background in herbal medicine.

Try meditation as part of tip number six. Although we have already talked about meditation, I

believe it is still important to mention it. We can gain a lot of advantages from meditation. One is undoubtedly increased focus and concentration. A study that emphasized awareness and greater attentiveness was carried out in 2011. The study caused people's memory and other cognitive capacities to increase.

Another thing to realize is that meditation does not necessarily include just sitting still and closing your eyes. While meditating, you can engage in a variety of activities such as yoga and deep breathing. I implore you to pause right now and practice meditation. On your quest to draw the situations you want, this is one of the most exceptional abilities you can have.

A break is the seventh piece of advice. Sometimes, keeping your attention on a stressful situation can have the opposite impact of what you want. It might seem counterintuitive to take a break.

But it works. It can help you focus and consider other solutions to an issue if you leave a scenario for even five minutes and then return.

Eighth tip: Enjoy some music or sound. While working or studying, playing music can help you focus more. If you don't want to listen to music while you work, think about employing nature sounds or doing anything else you can to block off background noise. Your ability to focus will increase and your brain's ability to work at its best will be enabled.

According to certain research, the kind of music you listen to can also have an impact. The best music to listen to improve attention, according to experts, is either classical music or nature sounds.

Try trying electronic music or ambient music without lyrics if you don't like classical music or nature sounds. Keep the music low or at background noise volume to prevent it from becoming a distraction. It's also crucial to keep in mind that listening to music you love or detest will ultimately divert your attention.

Changing up your diet is our tenth piece of advice. Similar to how they alter your vibrations, the things you eat have an impact on your memory and focus. Avoiding processed meals, and sugary, greasy, or fatty foods is essential. Excellent nutrients for the brain include spinach, blueberries, fish, and eggs. Additionally, drinking plenty of water will help you focus and concentrate. Even minor dehydration might make it harder for a person to concentrate or focus.

Tenth tip: If you don't want to, we are not advocating that you include coffee in your diet. However, some research suggests that consuming caffeine might help with attention and focus, so if you feel as though your focus is waning or you are having trouble concentrating, you might want to try a cup of tea or coffee. According to a 2017 study, the naturally occurring phytochemicals in matcha, a type of green tea, not only serve to promote relaxation but also enhance cognitive performance. This can make it a fantastic alternative if coffee doesn't agree with your system.

Try some supplements is the next piece of advice we offer. Some dietary supplements encourage better concentration and brain health. Of course, speak with your doctor before taking supplements, especially if you have worries about existing medical conditions or allergies. The ideal person to discuss the benefits and risks you might encounter is your health care provider, who can also suggest the most suitable options for your requirements.

Getting all the vitamins you require each day from your diet alone is not always an option. Supplements can fill in the gaps left by your diet in this situation. Supplements containing choline, flavonoids, folate, guarana seed extract, omega-3 fatty acids, and vitamin K are frequently linked to improved focus and attention.

Try practicing your concentration, advice number twelve. Those who have trouble focusing will benefit greatly from this kind of exercise. This is a mental exercise that entails giving something your entire attention for a set amount of time. These exercises for improving concentration may include some of the following:

- Set a timer for three to five minutes, and make an effort to blink as little as possible during that period.

- Draw or doodle for 15 minutes while the timer is set.

- Hold onto a companion and throw a balloon or small ball back and forth.

- Obtain a hard candy or lollipop, and consume it completely. You have to fight the impulse to bite into this one. Pay attention to the flavor, the way the candy feels on your tongue, and how long it takes you to finish it.

After finishing these tasks, consider your feelings regarding the event. Analyze the emotions you felt, the times you lost focus, and how you were able to regain them. Also, consider the feelings you had.

It seems to sense that some conditions can make it difficult to focus. The events going on around you can also make it difficult to focus.

Concentration lapses frequently result from interruptions from coworkers, social media messages, or even interruptions from family members.

However, it's also possible that the person's underlying physical or mental health issues are the cause of their attention problems. ADHD, cognitive dysfunction or impairment, depression or anxiety, concussions, or vision issues may be among them.

Regardless of age, people with attention-deficit/hyperactivity disorder frequently struggle with learning and memory issues. It frequently exhibits a pattern of inattention, impulsivity, and sometimes even hyperactivity. If you believe that ADHD is stopping you from being able to concentrate or focus, you should speak with a health care provider. There are various treatment options available for those who suffer from ADHD.

Developmental delays or disabilities can frequently be a symptom of a separate cognitive dysfunction or impairment that impairs your ability to focus, learn, or remember things. You can use some techniques to support this cognitive focus.

Finding the best way to improve your function and productivity requires speaking with a health care professional to develop a plan of action.

When your mood or emotion fluctuates, you could experience anxiety or despair. These emotions may make it difficult for you to concentrate or focus. You must identify the underlying causes of your anxiety or depression. You can't always accomplish this on your own. You might need to go to a therapist for expert assistance. However, it is unlikely that you will be able to focus and create the things you want until you address whatever is impeding your capacity to concentrate or figure out how to live with your anxiety.

Concentration and memory are frequently impacted in those who have experienced head trauma or concussions. Although it rarely lasts longer than a few hours, this could happen while the concussion is healing. It is crucial that you collaborate with your doctor during this time to make sure you are healing properly and that your injury isn't causing any additional cognitive problems.

Farsightedness or other visual issues are other factors that aren't as well known but can have an impact on our ability to concentrate. These may make it more difficult for someone to focus or pay attention.

People who have it frequently report having frequent headaches and frequently squinting. Make an appointment to have your eyes checked if you think this might be a barrier for you. Your capacity to focus and concentrate could significantly change if you wear glasses.

These are just a few pointers to help you focus better. It's time to seek a piece of professional advice if you discover that things are not functioning for you. You are a unique individual, and there may be something out of the norm that is deterring you and impairing your ability to concentrate or focus that you are not yet aware of.

A crucial first step is to ask a therapist for help. It can be challenging for you to identify these items if you are exhibiting symptoms of severe stress. Here is where a qualified expert can intervene and identify indications that you might be missing. It is possible to have ADHD and struggle with having trouble focusing for extended periods even as an adult. Working with a mental health expert can help you determine whether you have this problem and the best course of action for you.

The basic line is that there are techniques for enhancing focus and attention. Finding the approach that will work best for you is crucial even though some work better than others.

Which approaches are the most effective is still a hot topic of discussion. However, there is strong evidence to support the idea that engaging in mental exercise helps enhance concentration. If nothing else, these suggestions are unlikely to harm your ability to concentrate. So, trying them out will only be to your advantage. However, it is always better to speak with your healthcare provider if you have any worries.

How to Conquer Fear and Make It a Source of Strength

One thing is certain: since emotions are irrational, fear cannot be vanquished by reason.

This same logic must be applied to direct emotional energy constructively to stop instinctive reactions before panic attacks.

In this manual, I explain how to transform fear into power and offer a quick, doable exercise to free the mind and conquer even the most terrifying anxieties.

Fear: ally or enemy?

Our survival depends on the basic emotion of fear, especially when it is associated with genuine dangers.

When fear is suppressed or rejected, it might cause an underestimation of prospective threats and significant risk exposure. In other situations, if fear is not successfully controlled, the risks may be exaggerated and fear may give rise to panic.

Beyond the realm of possibility, trying to eradicate fear from our lives would be immensely detrimental.

You will gain a useful ally and be able to take advantage of her energy if you can regard her as a buddy who comes to your aid.

This is not always simple, though, as fear is a very strong feeling that frequently gets you into problems. Because of this, anxiety and panic disorders are very common in our culture.

How can one prevent fear?

How can fear be overcome by courage?

The first step in finding the answers to these questions is to comprehend how our bodies and minds respond to terror triggers.

What unintentional mistakes are made the most frequently?

- Overcoming panic: When fear causes you to become uncontrollable.

- Tips for dealing with panic attacks.

Our minds are wired to predict and prepare for potential threats. This autonomic system works to keep us safe and secure our survival.

Due to this, the mind constantly has negative, frequently catastrophic ideas and fears if it is not educated.

The real issue arises when you take these thoughts seriously and develop a phobia of the bodily symptoms that accompany terror.

In actuality, fear sets off a physiological response in our bodies that, in the event of danger, predisposes us to attack or flee. When faced with a threat, this adrenaline rush enables us to act quickly to defend ourselves or flee.

The issue is that hazards we encounter daily frequently arise from our negative thoughts anticipating a potential threat in the future or right now.

Panic can sometimes strike out of nowhere. Our inner world is attempting to communicate with us. Perhaps it is telling us to make a change we have been putting off, to pay attention to an unmet need, or to give in to a suppressed desire.

What to do when the enemy is unseen in the age of the Coronavirus: managing terror.

Overcoming fear becomes more difficult in the current crises since it is triggered by outside forces from which there is no way to flee or protect oneself physically.

Therefore, in this instance, you may have a profound sense of dread and helplessness that runs the risk of obstructing or training the mind to the point that you are unable to go about your regular activities calmly.

It is crucial to understand that emotional responses taken to lessen the agitation brought on by negative thoughts are more likely to create anxiety.

Control or repression are frequently used as these problematic responses.

Here's how to identify the most common errors, prevent them, and transform anxiety into inner power.

Control attempts that result in loss of control

When one is terrified of one's feelings, the first mistake is to perform control rituals to reduce the physical symptoms of worry and fear.

However, because they are uncontrollable due to their spontaneity, you run the risk of escalating them if you try to suppress them.

In reality, attempts to manage their work in the opposite direction of the desired result since having too much control causes you to become uncontrollable. This is how panic develops from fear.

How can I manage my anxiety about being sick and my hypochondria?

Even with the greatest of intentions, acting impulsively could have disastrous results and make matters worse.

When someone is afraid of being sick, for instance, they may start looking online for diagnoses of any symptoms they may be experiencing. This just serves to increase their anxiety, set off a state of panic, and fill their head with unending worries.

These dangers provide a stressful and tense psycho-physical environment that strengthens the immune system's weak points.

- The unfavorable effect of acting out of fear is that you run the chance of having your fears come true.

- Even with the best of intentions, bad things happen.

- Why is this happening, exactly?

- Is it feasible to stop these negative actions?

- the mind to be unlocked and directed toward positive activities, the next step must be understood.

- How to control strong emotions and irrational urges. Be aware of your fears and face them. The first thing to keep in mind is that we often overlook long-term threats in favor of immediate danger.

Because of this, when you experience intense emotions, you typically try to release anxiety through impulsive acts that are frequently unreasonable and stronger than your own will.

Compared to the intricate procedures of rational thought, emotions are located in various parts of the brain where they are much more direct and primal.

This is how one runs the danger of acting impulsively by engaging in behavioral dynamics that only serve to exacerbate the problem.

The true cause of impulsive and instinctive emotional reactions is that when emotion takes control, we fail to consider the repercussions of our choices.

Awareness is the only tool that can stop impulsive behaviors.

The only way to prevent emotional responses that are likely to make matters worse is to consider the long-term effects of your actions.

turning fear into confidence and overcoming it.

It can be debilitating to think that you can't accomplish something, that you're not capable of doing it, or that you don't have the resources.

This limiting belief's worst effect is to prevent any attempts to take action against an unpleasant circumstance, running the risk of having to endure it quietly.

We can only face and control fear if we confront it.

If we don't do this, denying or suppressing it, we run the risk of letting fear lead us in the exact opposite direction of where we want to go.

Fear has the power to spur change.

More than desire, fear can motivate us to take the required steps to bring about improvement.

The only way out is to harness the emotional charge of fear toward taking wise and useful acts.

Don't let your fear paralyze you; only by understanding the true threat can you avoid it.

Your anxieties will become stronger if you try to run from or suppress them. They will make you stronger if you embrace them, meet them head-on, and intensify them.

How to get over your worst fear: a real-world workout (in 2 steps)

How to deal with your worst fear. You can perform this exercise whenever you have anxiety, agony, dread, or concern, but I advise you to do so right away to experience its "pleasant effects".

The first thing to do is to face your fear.

Take five or ten minutes to freely reflect on your scariest fear while sitting comfortably.

Which idea or imagination sets it off the most?

Imagine your greatest nightmare, knowing that nothing bad can ever happen to you. Try to picture every element as though you were experiencing the scene from a movie.

Look at its face instead of rejecting it or fleeing. Pause to pay attention to it.

Do you sense fear's electricity pulsing through your body?

Stay with this sensation for a while.

Try to intensify it, to feel it more strongly, as if you wanted to turn up the volume, rather than reject it. Keep thinking about your darkest fantasy to accomplish this; it will help if you close your eyes.

Although 30 minutes is the ideal amount of time to perform this exercise, you can try it out for only five minutes at first.

The second step is to free your mind and direct your energies.

What could you see or hear?

Is the risk you anticipated real? Or did your mind overstate the risks, making them appear almost extreme now?

Try asking yourself: If I wanted to make my biggest fear come true, what should I do (or not do) as of today? if you feel that the risk is genuine or likely.

Then develop a list of the things you could do to intentionally worsen the situation and bring about the worst-case scenario you imagined during the exercise.

Keep in mind that there are only two ways to respond to fear: either risk experiencing it (without intending to) or become aware of it and steer clear of it.

The only time you can change your course and head on a more constructive path is after you've recognized the "false steps."

Learn how to use your emotions to your advantage.

It will be more apparent to you if you have read this far and tried the exercise I suggested that:

You must learn to control impulses that are driven by inner forces that are far stronger than willpower if you want to control your emotions. You must get to know your emotional energy to understand how to control it and channel it efficiently and productively.

- Accepting fear is a prerequisite for developing courage.

- To prevail, pain must be crossed.

- For anger to be productive, it must be controlled.

Do not be afraid of your emotions; they are there to support you rather than weaken you.

For my part, it's important to clarify that, in some circumstances, you could want a led path to assist you in quickly dispelling your worry, panic, and anxieties using techniques suited to your particular situation.

Prosperity and Plenty

Did you know that every day, you have many thoughts running through your head? Do you comprehend how these thoughts can shape your reality? Did you know that by reorganizing and sharpening these thoughts to clarify what you want in life, you can change your future? It is not that they are not as fortunate as the wealthy or that they have not had enough opportunity to make money that most people are not as wealthy as they think they should be. Simply put, it's because their energies don't support abundance. If you have negative associations with or notions about money, you don't have a wealth mindset.

We already spoke about how some people develop the belief that "money is the source of all evil" or that "money is not significant in life." If you genuinely think that having money is difficult or the root of all evil, you are not setting yourself up for success in achieving wealth. One of my friends held the opinion that everyone who is affluent has scammed someone to get there. He always lacked money, as one could expect. Because he had negative associations or views about money, he was unable to attract wealth.

Before continuing to read, take a moment to consider your ideas on money. You will need to undergo a paradigm change if you believe that money is bad or difficult to obtain.

You are not attracting wealth into your life if you believe that having money makes individuals selfish and pompous.

Again, I am aware of those folks who constantly bemoan their plight. They discuss their inability to make ends meet or how they never seem to have enough money. They frequently ponder how some people appear to be flush with cash. The approach and perspective you take on money make a difference.

You will only attract more poverty if you concentrate on being poor. You will continue to experience that need in your life if you are continually preoccupied with it.

Let's use the comparison of the statements "I wish to be rich, wealthy, and prosperous" and "I don't want to be destitute, desperate, and lonely" as an example. It is not, however, the same.

They are complete opposites in the mind's subconscious. The first discusses wealth, whereas the second is concerned with poverty. In contrast to the second, which is about "not wanting," the first "acts and talks" about something.

The subconscious mind doesn't hear negativity, as I have mentioned.

In the first statement, it understands money, wealth, and prosperity; in the second, it understands poverty, desperation, and solitude. Use the law of attraction correctly if you want to bring abundance or create prosperity. Start imagining prosperity as a flow of energy into your life. You'll be astounded at how effortless the wealth-building process may be.

Financial Mindset

If you want to use the law of attraction, you must have the appropriate money attitude. What is the proper financial mindset? Continually consider money to attract money? Yes. Your views on money, however, shouldn't be unbiased. For instance, you can be required to make a certain amount of money from a project or to save XYZ amount every six months. These are cold, hard facts about money that might not help you attract more money into your life.

Use your judgment when it comes to making money. Money should be viewed as a tool, not as an aim in itself. Consider the actions you should do to draw in money. Consider the worth or caliber of your job, service, or product. Consider the items that will increase your wealth. Maintaining focus on the quality of your goods or services will increase sales, which will lead to more prospects for wealth accumulation.

A person who practices the law of attraction does not believe they must sell something to gain money. Instead, he or she believes that "I must provide my customers with solid value to generate money" or "I must know how to build the best product or service to make my customers' lives simple."

The best way to attract wealth is to have that money mindset. Put your attention on providing value or on your plans for making money. Rather than approaching the topic of wealth creation objectively, this will take care of the issue.

You will come up with quick-fix wealth-building solutions that won't work in the long run if you simply worry about the money and not the method through which you will accumulate riches. On the other side, when you concentrate on how to produce money or develop wealth, you are concentrating on making money morally and honestly. When you have faith in the law of attraction to create wealth, you develop an honesty that makes it easier for you to understand what it takes to draw money.

Strong Money Manifestation Advice

1. Trust! The first step in triggering the law of attraction is believing. You must first have the belief that you can attract prosperity, abundance, and money into your life. You must have faith in your ability to prosper and think that you are deserving. You should have ingrained in your psyche the idea of prosperity. You must believe that you will experience financial success and prosperity in your life. Imagine you are already prosperous, wealthy, and successful.

Operating from a mindset of the scarcity of wealth will only make poverty and lack of resources worse. The goal is to think of what you want as being a done deal—something that is completely assured to be yours. You won't be able to invoke the law of attraction until then. Work your emotions into believing that you are affluent, even if it is not real. If you believe that something you want is already yours, your sensations, ideas, and emotions will manifest more readily. Align your feelings and thoughts with money. Imagine what it would be like to be affluent. Consider the feelings and thoughts you will experience after you are wealthy.

2. Harness the power of visualization to draw in the things you want. Create your future by projecting using your thoughts. Create mental pictures of achieving your goal.

Keep in mind that you are not a mere bystander to the movie. You are acting out the part that you want to do in your life. You can picture yourself getting the outcomes you want.

You see yourself enjoying a drink on a secluded beach while on vacation with your family or sipping coffee next to the fireplace in your ideal home. You're in the car of your dreams. What is the feel of the steering wheel in your hand? When you sit down on the seats, how do you feel? How does the car feel when it gains speed? Imagine, sense, and drive the car of your dreams. Imagine yourself achieving the outcomes you want.

Imagine yourself at your dream location if you want to earn more money to visit the world. How does it feel to travel around those neighborhoods and explore those locations? To fully experience a place, engage all of your senses. Think about how much money you want. Don't consider it something you will receive in the future. See it right now in your bank account. Feel the feelings one has when they have a specific sum of money in their bank account.

Feel the emotions of having a million bucks in your account even though you have almost nothing. Although it is difficult, it is not impossible. This is precisely why some people are effective at using the law of attraction to their advantage while others are perplexed as to why they are unable to get the desired effects. See those $1,000,000 or $10,000,000 in your account right now, not in the future.

Feel the same feelings you would if you had a million or ten million dollars in your bank account. I would suggest taking it a step further and beginning your financial planning (this is a little-known suggestion). When we have money, we generally behave in this manner. Consider your investment or spending options.

Visualize the money while thinking along such lines.

The family of a young boy who lived in extreme poverty for much of his childhood once occupied a trailer that was parked on a relative's lawn. He worked eight-hour hours at the nearby factory after school just to support his family. Due to financial difficulties, the young man had to leave high school and start working odd jobs to help his family. He tried modest stand-up comedy performances because he couldn't support the whole family, but he failed there!

The young man, fed up with his lot in life, traveled to Hollywood at the age of 21 with hopes of becoming wealthy and escaping his miserable way of life. He did something upon arriving in Hollywood that affected the rest of his life. He parked his rusty Toyota in the Hollywood Hills so he could enjoy the vistas of the glittering lights of Tinseltown sweeping before him like a dream coming true. He imagined himself as a comedian in that glitzy entertainment industry, making people laugh.

He wanted a physical memento of this moment—a moment that would continuously drive him toward recognition and success—rather than just envisioning it. He quickly pulled out his checkbook and wrote a ten-million-dollar cheque for himself. His present bank balance was far from that amount. But he wrote down the precise sum because he wanted a concrete reminder of his achievement. The check was for "acting services rendered" and it was dated ten years in the future.

As a constant reminder of his objectives, he kept them in his wallet. He carried the check in his wallet wherever we went, whether it was for a meeting or an audition. The young man, who was extremely confident that it would only be a matter of time before he manifested the then million dollars, threw the check in his father's coffin when he passed away.

The actor did receive a sizable signing bonus for his future movie, and he finally went on to earn the ten million dollars he had been forecasting. Jim Carrey, an actor, was the young guy who signed a ten million dollar check to himself that night on Hollywood Hills. This is the power of visualizing, believing, and imagining that something is already yours before it is.

3. even though you may not seem to have much, be thankful for what you do have. You must be thankful for what you already have to build more in the future. There are few odds of you generating more of what you want if you don't look at what you have with some gratitude. Thank the universe for providing you with money because when you are thankful for what you currently have, such as wealth and things, you will draw in even more of what you want.

Don't limit your gratitude to tomorrow. Show appreciation for what you already have as well. If you want to build the future of your desires, imagine feeling grateful for the present. Your energy of gratitude for abundance increases when your thoughts and feelings line up with a sincere sense of thanksgiving, which helps you attract even more abundance! To assist you to attract anything you desire, you are sharing universal rules.

4. Be tenacious. Pursue your goals with zeal and persistence!

Don't give up at any point. There will be obstacles in your path.

Move past them to get closer to your objectives. Never stop taking action or pursuing your goals. It is insufficient to simply visualize your ambitions and goals. Daily action must be taken to further these objectives. What actions did you take today to move closer to your goal? Stopping or pausing indicates that you are worn out and frail, which will not assist you in attracting the prosperity and abundance you desire.

Don't let your trembling beliefs' vibrations be picked up by the universe. Tell the cosmos that you're going to keep going. If you take the appropriate actions, riches will eventually find their way into your life. Your self-assurance signals to the universe that you are open to receiving anything you desire and that you are prepared to put in the necessary effort to amass prosperity and abundance.

5. Strike a balance between inner quiet and external action. Creating a balance between our inner and outer selves is one of the little-known yet incredibly effective concepts of the law of attraction. What is referred to as consciousness is your inner self. It has to do with how you behave and think. What is displayed to the outside world, is strongly related to your outward self or external energy.

We try to affect a change in our inner selves or minds through the law of attraction. We use our emotions, ideas, and feelings to do this. Through the influence of our thoughts and images, we construct or project a future in our minds. Our outside self consists of activity, but our inner self consists of thinking. Our exterior functions are determined by how we put our thoughts into practice. It's crucial to strike a balance between your inner and outer selves if you want to fully benefit from the persuasive law of attraction. Without doing an action that is consistent with your thoughts, simply thinking about something all day won't bring it to you.

When you consider prosperity and abundance, you must also take the appropriate steps to support your thoughts. You need to act upon what you think. The law of attraction's fundamental idea is that. You plant the seed of an idea in your mind, and then you grow it by turning these ideas into deeds. For the law of attraction to work, certain conditions must be met. The universe's duty is made easier by the alignment of internal and external energy since it helps you achieve your goals.

Make sure your behaviors are in line with your goals. If you have an impulse to do anything, it should line up with your thoughts and feelings. The secret to making the law of attraction truly work for you is to strike a balance between your internal sense of stillness and your outward behaviors. You might consider manifesting a new house or car.

However, unless it is supported by corresponding activities, simply thinking and forming thoughts about it is insufficient. If you genuinely trust in the power of the cosmos, then things will naturally align themselves toward manifesting. However, you must start the momentum by acting in some way to achieve your objectives.

Despite receiving a check for $10 million, Jim Carrey didn't just sit around doing nothing. He aggressively attended meetings and auditions, according to him (and he always had the magic check in his wallet). These possibilities, which he actively sought out, helped him manifest the $10 million. He coordinated his energy for wealth building with action.

Strong ideas and deeds elicit responses from the universe. To get where you want to go in life, take the initiative and strive toward your dreams. You own the power to get the outcomes you want. Use your inner self to have faith in and conviction about your goals, and your outer self to aggressively pursue them. If you want to realize your dreams, there should be a balance or combination of the two. When you believe in something, put it into practice, and achieve it, your odds of receiving a response from the universe grow dramatically.

Acting will teach your mind to strive for these objectives. They will be pursued by the subconscious mind like puppies following a string ball. If you train your subconscious mind to think in terms of wealth generation, you will advance along the road to riches and prosperity more quickly. Consider all the lovely pictures you see in travel publications. It features images of a faraway white sand beach, lush fields, or a vast blue sky with an empty chair in the distance.

Your attention is drawn to the vacant chair. Subconsciously, it desires to sit on the chair. Our objectives are essentially the same. Where you are and where you desire to differ from each other. Just like we are drawn to our goals, your mind is drawn to the chair. The distance between where you are right now and where you want to be can be filled with the aid of the law of attraction.

6. Dispel any misconceptions, biases, and mental barriers you may have regarding money. If you think negatively about money, your internal antenna isn't tuned to the appropriate frequency. You can't play the appropriate visuals on television if you can't pick up the right frequency. A bad wire or failure to pick up the proper frequency are the main causes of the picture's increased sporadicness. When it comes to applying the law of attraction, there is a lot of prejudice that stands in the way. I know a lot of people who want the law to work its magic, yet they are held back by their negative attitudes and prejudices about wealth. To make getting money easier and more favorable, cultivate a more optimistic view of wealth.

7. See energy in money. Forget about your earnings, expenses, and debt. All of these are just energy. Neither of them is adverse nor favorable. They are ultimately just energy, which is neutral and based on science. You are reacting to or vibrating in response to an energy force. Instead of perceiving money as the sum of its parts and trying to possess it all, viewing it as energy can boost your chances of attracting it.

8. Avoid comparing yourself to others. Comparing one's life and journey with others is the biggest barrier to creating money through the law of attraction. So and so has a lot of money, but I'm still having trouble making ends meet. Do not contrast your path or fate with those of others. You must

pursue your path and destiny. Additionally, feeling jealous of someone else's plenty will make it impossible for you to attract wealth.

Never feel resentment or jealousy for someone else's achievement or money. In this way, money does not make you feel good. You believe it is difficult for you to obtain money while being simple for others. This is precisely the message you send to the universe, which prevents you from pursuing wealth creation simply or easily (just in line with your pessimistic beliefs about earning money). Always be joyful and optimistic about the wealth of others.

Believe that everyone has access to money. You won't necessarily become impoverished just because someone else received a rise. Genuinely rejoice for the fortunate, and you'll see a change in your prosperity. If you work to connect your emotions and energies with the cosmos, you will experience abundance because the universe is bountiful.

There is plenty for everyone, and everyone has the power to bring money, riches, prosperity, and abundance into their lives.

9. You get more by giving more. Even if you do not have enough, you are acting from a position of abundance when you offer riches or money. You are telling the universe that you are wealthy enough to share with others. Giving to charity isn't it thought of as a sign of affluence and success? The universe sends you even more abundance when you project positive energy related to riches and abundance.

Giving is therefore one of the most effective methods to use the law of attraction to attract prosperity.

Growth Mindset

Even while change might be difficult, it is essential to our personal development. You should be willing to go above and beyond to develop habits and lifestyle patterns that will help you achieve your goals if you desire great rewards and magnificent things in your life.

Changing habits can occasionally be a mammoth undertaking. Most people might not be motivated or have a specific goal in mind when they decide to change long-standing habits.

However, it's imperative to break old poor habits and adopt new ones if you want to achieve success in all areas of your life.

Break a bad habit pattern, give yourself praise for good behavior, and make sure your activities are in line with your objectives. Habits affect how we live. Consistent behavior develops into habits, and these habits can affect our future. Which phase of creating a new habit presents the greatest difficulty? First month! The hardest obstacle to overcome is the initial inertia. Do not prepare yourself for the change by being anxious.

Recognize that sometimes to receive something worthwhile, you must give something up permanently. Avoid making a lot of abrupt changes. Go slowly in the proper direction. Step by step, steadily moving forward. When you make one positive step in the correct direction, it inspires you to make more. Let's say, for illustration purposes, that you wish to lose 40 pounds. Making drastic adjustments to your life won't result in big outcomes that appear overnight. It is not sustainable, healthy, or advised.

You'll start by making minor adjustments to your everyday routine, such as clearing out the junk food from your shelves and fitting in a quick workout each day. This can gradually be increased to include joining a weight loss program or diet and going to the gym. It is simpler to maintain moving in the right direction once you see results. Take bigger moves once you feel comfortable with the initial modifications.

Till you reach your goal, proceed with patience and tenacity. Change your poor habits for positive ones to advance yourself. Establishing brand-new, positive behaviors will aid in your personal growth.

Here are a few good habits that were designed to help you achieve your objectives.

1. Keep up with a daily exercise routine to improve your metabolism, physical fitness, mental acuity, and attention. It doesn't have to be a boring gym session. Getting moving for 30 to 60 minutes can be as enjoyable as dancing, cycling, or swimming.

You'll feel better about yourself, look better, and your stress level will go down as a result. Include physical activity in your daily routine.

2. Invest to increase your understanding of your field or industry.Read books written by motivational writers or professionals who have achieved significant success in your area. Read blogs and articles written by influential bloggers. Listen to audio programs and podcasts. Join seminars and professional networking events to meet individuals in your industry. Learn new concepts, themes, and inspiration sources.

3. Arrange your belongings to better manage your time.

Clearing out the clutter in your home is a good place to start. Things that bring up terrible memories or items that are no longer useful should not be kept. You'll find things more quickly and effectively if you get rid of unnecessary items. Schedule your time. Spend less time online or idly browsing social media. Get rid of time-consuming clubs, subscriptions, and acquaintances who don't enhance your life. Talk to people and focus your efforts on activities that will move you closer to your objective. Never forget: anything you give your attention to will expand.

4. Show your artistic side. No matter how busy you are, never be afraid to express your creativity. Not only is using your creativity an outlet for stress and therapy, but it also improves your ability to solve problems. I have met people whose lives have changed for the better as a result of taking up a passion like gardening, cooking, writing, or painting. Anything is possible, from knitting to photography to decorating to cooking.

Discover your calling and start today! A fantastic method to activate good behaviors, ideas, and intentions to draw more positivity into your life is to do something you are passionate about. Take a look at this awesome book on making money doing what you love!

5. Offer to help. Get involved with your neighborhood, a global group, or any NGO that champions a cause you care deeply about. When you devote your time and resources to a worthwhile cause, you experience a powerful uplift. There is great joy and delight in knowing that you even slightly improved someone's life or made them smile.

Additionally, working with those who are less fortunate will teach you to recognize your blessings and to express deeper thankfulness for what you have. You will have a beneficial impact on other people's lives, and as everything in the universe is related, this will also have a positive impact on your own life.

6. Take in some music. You may be able to unwind, recover, regenerate, and have fun with music. Create a lovely music collection with a variety of tunes to suit various moods and feelings. When you just want to get up and dance or when you need a boost of energy, have a few party music handy. Play moving music that inspires you. Put on some calming music and meditate when you need to relax.

7. Consume wholesome, well-balanced meals. Use the 80/20 rule when it comes to your diet! 80 percent of the time, you should eat healthfully, and for the remaining 20 percent, you should indulge. Reduce your intake of packaged, high-calorie junk food with artificial sweeteners. Opt for wholesome, uncomplicated, and fresh cuisine instead.

You'll be able to preserve your energy and avoid being lethargic, which will help you stay upbeat. What we eat has a direct impact on how we feel. If you consume high-fiber, high-nutrition meals, you'll experience less mental and physical exhaustion. This can help you maintain a happier outlook throughout the day. Concentrate on choosing healthy foods, but occasionally allow yourself some wiggle room.

8. Refrain from hanging out with negative or energy-draining folks.

These are the people who will drain you of all of your positive energy. They'll make fun of your objectives. They'll be complaining and whining to you all the time. Remove them from your life's narrative. Instead, surround yourself with upbeat and joyful individuals. It doesn't take long for mentality and energy to spread from one person to another.

Spending time with someone who constantly tells you that your goals are unattainable, that you are inadequate, or that the world is a dreadful place may cause you to frequently adopt their pessimistic viewpoints. Avoid spending time with people who dismiss your ambitions as unattainable, sympathize with you, speak poorly of others, or complain nonstop about various things.

9. Never cease investing in yourself. Do whatever you can to develop your personality, learn new skills, and increase your knowledge. Consider picking up a new skill, enrolling in a new class, returning to school, changing your wardrobe, learning a new language, taking a public speaking class to gain more

confidence, taking a cooking class, or learning a new skill.

It is evident when you invest in yourself. You not only get new talents but also a lovely sense of self-worth. This encourages more optimism and draws more favorable circumstances your way. Give yourself enough time to grow personally. It will affect both your present and future quality of life.

10. Get enough rest. Do not skimp on your sleep. You might not be aware of this right away. However, as your body ages, the effects and health risks become more apparent. A minimum of seven to eight hours of sleep every day are necessary. When you don't get enough sleep, you not only feel mentally and physically worn out but also in a more pessimistic frame of mind.

11. Rise and shine. If you ask the majority of successful people what their time management motto is, they'll probably respond to get up early and get ready for the day's work the night before.

Prepare everything for the next day before you go to sleep so that you don't have to spend time looking for things like your clothing or a crucial file. You may start right away and save time when everything is prepared, readily available, and your day has been properly planned. This will help you have a good day, lessen your tension, and maintain a positive attitude throughout the day.

12. Hiring a personal coach is among the best things you can do for your personal development. You may maintain inspiration, motivation, purpose, and

accountability with the aid of a personal coach. They will gently nudge you back on course if you stray from your objectives. You can maintain your focus firmly fixed on optimism and important things by taking into account a qualified coach's perspective.

13. Devote time to introspection. Enjoy some private time with yourself. Spend some time considering your ideas, objectives, and behavior. You hear other people talking throughout the day. Spend some downtime tuning into your inner voice, subconscious thoughts, and instincts.

Exercise, meditate, pray, recite affirmations or mantras, keep a journal, practice yoga—do whatever it takes for you to connect with your inner self.

Sometimes you want to communicate your deepest emotions and feelings without telling anyone else. To feel more optimistic and at ease, record them in a notebook.

Taking Action Psychosomatic illnesses and self-healing

And despite all of this discussion, only a select minority succeed in learning and using efficient self-healing methods.

Let's start with the cause of the bodily imbalance—the disease, the pathology, or the unintentional event—before discussing how to repair yourself with your mind.

The majority of the illnesses that plague us have a genesis or at the very least a "psychosomatic" component, according to my perspective, which is becoming more and more prevalent even in medical-scientific surroundings.

Our mind will be less likely to activate defenses against external agents if it is stressed and we feel fatigued, tense, or restless, leaving us more vulnerable to attack.

I think that even unintentional occurrences like a car accident, a slip, and fall, or an injury typically have links to unconscious motivations that are always controlled by our mind and that have exposed us to external risk factors and have induced the circumstance that led to the trauma.

In other words, according to the most recent theories of Mental Dynamics, to which the Sailfulness Method relates, the relationships between the mind, body, events, diseases, and healing can be harmoniously structured, significantly extending and especially improving people's quality of life. and put them at less risk, even unintentional risk.

When things are out of balance, the mind may even start a pathology, keeping us, so to speak, "safe" from a stressful circumstance.

Consider someone who goes to work every day feeling stressed about their bad employer. In these circumstances, a subconscious process that lowers the defenses is activated.

These individuals are 'physically' ill. Then the sickness with the accompanying fever becomes the excuse to take two days off work and avoid seeing the person who is so resented.

Through a variety of glands, our body creates chemicals with active ingredients that are quite comparable to many of the medications we take, but it may also concentrate on poisons and tensions that have effects that are very similar to those of the illnesses that affect us.

Placing a Belief

The Placebo Effect and its connection with Mental Dynamics techniques must be briefly discussed when discussing self-healing and healing with the mind.

Clinical studies that have been validated demonstrate that a significant portion of patients recover when given a fictitious treatment, whether it be a glass of water with sugar masquerading as a potent anti-inflammatory or a mock surgery. What causes this to occur?

It is now commonly accepted that the placebo effect results from positive beliefs being triggered by pseudo-care, which alters the body's physiology.

We believe that the contrary is also true, a concept known as the "Nocebo Effect" by academics.

The detrimental physiological effects of the negative beliefs even make it more difficult for us to use our natural self-healing mechanisms.

To better grasp this idea, consider a straightforward example. According to some social norms, the standard response to the inane question "how are you" is "so-so," "let's get on with it," or "it's not bad." Some cultures, like Italian culture, are typically conservative and prudent.

One thing to remember: focus on the "not awful" in particular. The mind is easily tricked by negations, which are intricate abstractions, but it tends to concentrate on the word "evil," with all of its unfavorable connotations that are unaffected by the negation "there is not."

Avoiding double negations is one of the fundamental principles of mental dynamics, which helps to convert "there is no evil" into "good."

Returning to social customs, try asking "how are you?" in Manchester and the same question in Los Angeles to see which one is more appropriate. You'll find that the Americans will respond with "good!" or "excellent!" or "give me five!" or "wonderful!" while the British will typically respond with "not too bad."

Let's not be shocked if the Americans' optimistic outlook has propelled them to a dominant position in the world!

Therefore, the placebo effect is real, it is supported by science, and it can be triggered by a positive outlook, which each student will have mastered by the end of the Sailfulness Course.

Autoscopy

Our body is a sophisticated organism made up of numerous interconnected systems. Organs, the lymphatic and circulatory systems, the skeletal and muscular systems, and the nervous system...

We have developed extremely potent instruments to examine the architecture and physiology of each system and organ to diagnose and treat the numerous diseases that can affect our systems and organs. X-rays to MRI scans, CT scans to ultrasounds, and so on.

What if the mind could also transform into a highly potent scanner at our disposal, able to identify tensions, contractures, and other issues while simultaneously aiding in our physical well-being through the potent placebo effect that it may provide?

Use your thoughts to heal yourself

In the history of humanity, scientific medicine as we know it now is a relatively recent development.

People have relied on healers, sorcerers, and shamans for millennia, but their solutions, often herbal, were only tangentially tied to active principles of healing, leaving it to words, gestures, rituals, and recommendations to trigger people's innate healing abilities.

I do not want to downplay the value of contemporary medical science. It would be absurd to substitute an appeal to the ancestors' spirits for chemotherapy. However, it would be incredibly constricting to ignore the mind's basic significance for the self-healing processes.

It is possible to heal with the mind, and it can complement traditional medicine rather than replace it.

Self-healing methods can also help you manage your pain since they teach you how to live better even while you're ill or facing challenging circumstances. This goes beyond just using your mind to heal.

Medieval and contemporary medicine

From Chinese medicine (acupuncture) to Ayurveda, all forms of ancient medicine are founded on the idea of self-healing.

A natural approach to health is once again being discovered in modern times, especially at this time. More and more people are talking about naturopathy, herbal sciences, up to energy, and quantum medicine.

A more responsible attitude on the part of the individual toward his or her health has replaced the allopathic approach, which treats the disease's symptoms rather than its underlying cause.

A new (holistic) perspective holds that the source of the sickness should be looked for internally, as opposed to outside, and that the individual is an indivisible whole of body, mind, and spirit.

This information, which served as the foundation for ancient medicine, has long been taken into account by "official" medicine.

The link between our thoughts and emotions and health is confirmed by fields like psycho-neuro-endocrine-immunology (PNEI), which investigates the connection between the psyche and the immunological, endocrine, and neurological systems.

How can I encourage self-healing?

As we previously stated, self-healing is a normal and spontaneous process, but its potential may be compromised by a serious state of extreme bodily imbalance that makes it difficult or impossible for the body to initiate the process.

We can make use of some methods and best practices to preserve or encourage the restoration of our system's optimal settings.

Here are a few examples.

Nutrition

Without a doubt, health begins here. For the body to continue to operate well, proper nutrition is essential. It has been demonstrated, for instance, that maintaining an alkaline condition in the body is intimately related to one's level of health.

Additionally, the vegan and vegetarian diets have several additional advantages for maintaining good health.

We can rely on dietary supplements and superfoods in addition to food to maintain a decent level of energy and advance bodily health.

Rest

The brain eliminates extra toxins and balances the neurological system as you sleep. To feel well and keep the body from experiencing excessive stress, get enough sleep. The body becomes congested as a result of excessive stress and unexpelled pollutants, making it unable to carry out its normal activities.

It's crucial to keep your sleep cycle at seven to eight hours per night (or whatever your body requires).

Feelings and thoughts

Our ideas and emotions are other key factors that we must consider. Since many diseases have a psychosomatic cause, we are aware of the detrimental effects that thoughts and emotions can have on our health.

A cheerful attitude, self-control over one's thoughts, and the ability to express one's emotions all encourage self-healing and promote health.

When we know the power we possess, we can alter the status of our cells and even our DNA with nothing more than our thoughts, words, or actions.

disciplines and methods

We can maintain our health or speed up the healing process with the aid of many holistic disciplines and some spiritual practices. Here are a few examples:

Meditation - Research on meditation has revealed that it reduces stress and anxiety, fosters a calm calming, boosts vital energy, and aids in the healing process.

Reiki and Theta Healing

Using these approaches, we may rebalance energy and thoroughly address mental problems and energy barriers.

Tibetan ceremonies and yoga The Tibetan ceremonies also come from the ancient science of yoga, which is a practice to regulate the energy flow in our bodies and restore equilibrium to the body, mind, and spirit.

Acupuncture and reflexology are the foundations of traditional Chinese medicine for a long ago. By using a preventive strategy, these techniques help to keep the body healthy.

Essential oils and Bach Flowers When combined with specialized massage techniques, several beneficial naturopathic practices, including the use of essential oils and flower therapy, favor the health of the body and mind in a subtle yet significant way.

Listening to mantras, sound therapies, or music at particular sound frequencies (such as music at 432 Hz) might help bring the body and mind into internal harmony.

Many people have seen healings (natural or spontaneous) from even serious illnesses occur without the use of medications or standard medical procedures.

Even conditions deemed "incurable" by conventional medicine now have a cure, thanks to a new conception of health.

Self-healing = Healing

It would be sufficient to comprehend that we are ultimately responsible for everything that occurs to us and that we have the power to alter it.

In the end, we may conclude that healing is always susceptible to the mechanisms of self-healing because the individual plays such an important part in the healing process.

The body's intrinsic capacity to reestablish balance and health always serves as the foundation for healing, regardless of the drugs used or the nature of the healing activity.

10 Ways to Draw Abundance

1. The spiritual realm is the source of everything that occurs in the physical world.

If anything in our physical existence consumes a significant amount of our energy, it implies that the spiritual world has much to reveal as well.

If there are problems that make us work harder and push us toward \ something that seems unattainable... that challenge must be met, \sto attract much more energy into our lives! \s"

Do you feel that a certain event in your life is consuming a lot of your mental, physical, and spiritual energy? Or are you unsure whether to begin that project where you will accomplish something you love?

The same thing applies to your relationship, family, friends, and that girl (or guy) you adore but is giving you a hard time. I'm not just talking about money or a job here. In this instance, it indicates that the person genuinely cares about you and wants to put you to the test. Go ahead and act! Let's go for it! "

2. The cosmos wants to provide us with limitless wealth and enable us to automatically experience every form of blessing and prosperity.

Despite the universe's overall goodwill toward us, we set boundaries because we are terrified of gaining or losing limitless wealth.

Because of our ongoing anxiety, we have cut ourselves off from the universe.

We shall examine how to keep a consistent relationship with these heavenly riches in the following formulations.

As a result of our connection with the Universe, one of the energy containers that the Universe delivers to us is money.

When we have a lot of money, we feel secure, healthy, and full of energy. We also feel confident in ourselves and value ourselves, but what exactly is this sensation like?

True, abundant!

What I'm presenting you right now is a paradigm shift, a paradoxical idea—to live abundantly, you don't need money—which turns on our brains well.

(Abraham's and the Bible's period) looked like this

When you are committed to continuously establishing a connection with the universe and sharing your gifts with others, financial success is a given.

By doing this, you will also be equipped to maintain the steady cash flow that you are confident will occur.

This explains why people who play lotteries and lottos fall into poverty more and more—they are not utilizing their skills!

4. Money should be distributed to keep a steady cash flow!

Please wait!

Now that I've clarified that, let me emphasize that I'm not advocating gratuitous giving.

The human being, according to the Kabbalah, is like a pile; when we are in contact with the universe, energy flows and there is light; when we are cut off, there is confusion and darkness.

What can we do to continue to be in contact with the Light of the Universe without electrocuting ourselves?

Giving 10%, or the "tenth" of your income, is what Abraham did.

Here are some theories, both Catholic and Jewish, that are at odds with one another.

While other Kabbalists clarify that this is a "golden norm," certain Christian theologians argue that Abraham's practice of tithing was not usual.

If we check, there is a suggestion to give 10% of one's monthly income to charity under the "cans" strategy, which T. Harv Eker teaches in his Millionaire Mind Intensive program.

If he says so himself, it works.

When we learn to donate one-tenth to charity, this will be the positive pole connecting us to the universe, resulting in a constant flow of energy rather than an alternating one (money).

5. Our want to receive money is equal to and at odds with our desire to give it.

The energy that drives us to risk everything for ourselves, face our anxieties, dedicate ourselves to ourselves, and connect with the universe is real, but not because we are self-centered; rather, it is the exact opposite. It's the exact opposite!

let's start studying it (and putting it into practice) a little bit ourselves.

much money should we expect to earn during our lives?

INFINITE!

How much we can hold in our bodies is infinite "vase.

A human's desire to receive acts as a "vessel" for wealth and riches. Additionally, today we discovered that the ideal desire is to "receive and distribute

6. Your vase will be bigger and more ready to wisely receive all the riches of the world the more you want to "receive to share."

Why do 90% of lottery winners lose their money within a few months or years and are unhappy?

because of their selfish want.

7. The ego of someone who wants to live a "low profile" life is far larger than that of someone who wants all the riches in the world!

those who declare: "don't want to desire more because I am content with my current situation and don't need anything more. It is better not to devote yourself to that project that could take me around the world and introduce me to a wide range of fascinating and beautiful people, increasing my prosperity and that of those around me. It's preferable to stay at home, commute to that job I detest for 1000 euros a month, and keep silent because I could only end up getting lost."

They are secretly thinking, "I'm so terrified to leave and I envy those who manage to get rich, in my opinion, they are just people who steal, evildoers, better to play the lottery or purchase a scratch card," but they are not saying it out loud.

anything... scratch! (for anyone who wants to know how to draw a win)

Negative thoughts drag us down like lead!

Consider this!

8. To overcome unfavorable thoughts, it is important to understand what is restricting me. What are these beliefs?

To do this, we must acknowledge that sometimes we are the ones who hold back.

There is always an aspect of ourselves, which Kabbalists refer to as the "opponent," ready to limit our potential and prevent us from wanting to contribute more.

That voice there tells you: Sleep a little this morning...

Avoid going out with that person because you might fall head over heels in love. Don't do this because you might regret it "In other words, if we face our dark side, we have already completed half the task!

The expressions of our adversary are insecurity, blame, fear of failure, fear of success, and selfishness, which is the basis of all evil.

9. The secret is a certainty!

To change false notions and decide on confidence... The Kabbalists use "Hebrew letters" to do this.

One of the numerous ways to widen the heart and draw in increasing amounts of riches is to even embrace the trees!

10. To give while being conscious of receiving from the universe rather than the world!

Customers that pay you (from the World) are energy channels, and when you earn money, you are receiving energy from the Universe (from the Universe).

They decided to purchase your good or service because they perceived something of significant worth and utility in you.

They give you energy in exchange for money, which is only a vehicle because everything in the universe is interconnected like an electrical wire.

The choice is yours: disconnecting from the universe implies accepting chaos (an anagram of chance), and being connected to it means appreciating everything's perfection and magnificence (the great design of your life).

The sun provides life to the plant, the plant creates the flower, the flower pollinates the land, the earth joins the water, the water gives life to the plant that makes oxygen, and the oxygen allows humans to survive! In nature, there is no chaos; everything has its place.

And do you still think chaos is the natural state of life?

Conclusion

In a Heart Math study, participants were chosen at random to view a range of images on a screen. The participants' hearts' activity was monitored using meters that were attached to them. There was always a delay in between photos, and each time a bad image was about to be presented, the person's heart rate increased during the interval.

The study's finding was that the heart possesses an intuitive intelligence that is closely connected to our reality. The heart functioned almost like a warning system, sensing when something bad was about to happen.

Another piece of evidence from the field of epigenetics demonstrates how much the environment affects and has the power to change the genes that make up our DNA. Our DNA can be changed by the food we eat, the air we breathe, our habits, for better or worse, and even the way we regularly think. They have switch-like on/off capabilities. Multiple causes cause the genes that are passed down from generation to generation to change throughout time.

Therefore, the idea of passing down genes alone does not explain why children can adopt their parents' problems. The inheritance is more about sharing common surroundings, a common environment, a common diet, and a common way of thinking.

The point is that everything in our environment has an impact on our fields, which in turn impacts our bodies. Just as healthy food and a way of life can result in a healthy physique, our field governs us. Our lives design and what draws us to live a specific way are held in the deeper subconscious region that contains our mental routine programming.

Fortunately, everything exists on a spectrum, allowing the environment to shape who we are. By accepting the way things are, we can eventually use our ideas and feelings to influence the world around us.

So let's think about what we do know. Atoms are thought of as matter because of the electron field that surrounds them, which is a light particle. On rare occasions, the electron field collapses into an electron, a unit of substance.

The electron field collapses and transforms into a particle when human consciousness examines it, as demonstrated by the double slit experiment. These atoms and electrons are what make up our bodies. We may observe the idea of duality, solid and not solid, wave and particle, at this subatomic level.

Our consciousness breaks waves down into constituents. We are aware that every particle in the universe is interconnected, and that changing one particle leads to changing others. Every particle is linked. Time moves backward due to positrons. Our ability to feel other people's invisible fields is a function of our invisible fields, which are related to our intuition.

Our thoughts alone have the power to change our genes. We also know that everything vibrates constantly on a large and microscopic scale and that the planets themselves rotate in a forward direction.

As we can see, science provides us with numerous explanations for how our physical reality functions, yet only a select few scientific rules are accepted as being true by contemporary man. As I previously stated, science is still advancing, and in the grand scheme of things, it is still rather young.

The philosophers of ancient Egypt and Greece, on the other hand, were so perceptive of their world that they noticed things that science has only recently become aware of. As a result, esoteric laws have been known for ages, but they were only understood by the most affluent and well-educated people at the time.

Most people today have access to these laws thanks to the information age, but sadly, more people choose to use technology for entertainment rather than to learn from it.

We can give ancient laws new life and use them for our benefit by fusing modern scientific knowledge with ancient wisdom. Understanding and following these laws will make us all happier and more prosperous.

A number of these rules—many of which we have already discussed, thanks to Bob Proctor—are listed here, along with other older laws of life. They are the fundamental patterns that underlie how life functions and how they interact, demonstrating a straightforward symmetry. Here is a list of some of those rules along with how they relate to what we know about science today. One thing to keep in mind is that these principles apply to your life as well as the inner workings of life.